Giant's Dream

A healing journey through Nitassinan

NIKASHANT ANTANE

We gratefully acknowledge the financial support of the Canada Council for the Arts, the Government of Canada through the Canada Book Fund (CBF), and the Government of Newfoundland and Labrador through the Department of Tourism, Culture and Recreation for our publishing program.

Cover Design by Todd Manning
Layout by Joanne Snook-Hann and Todd Manning
Printed on acid-free paper

Published by
CREATIVE PUBLISHERS
an imprint of CREATIVE BOOK PUBLISHING
a Transcontinental Inc. associated company
P.O. Box 8660, Stn. A
St. John's, Newfoundland and Labrador A1B 3T7

Printed in Canada by:
TRANSCONTINENTAL INC.

Library and Archives Canada Cataloguing in Publication

Antane, Nikashant, 1959-
Giant's dream : a healing journey through Nitassinan / by Nikashant Antane.

ISBN 978-1-897174-53-1

1. Giant--Travel--Newfoundland and Labrador--Labrador. 2. Snowshoes and snowshoeing--Newfoundland and Labrador--Labrador. 3. Labrador (N.L.)--Description and travel. 4. Labrador (N.L.)--Pictorial works. I. Title.

FC2193.4.A58 2010 917.18'2045 C2010-900506-6

Giant's Dream

A healing journey through Nitassinan

St. John's, Newfoundland and Labrador
2011

For our relatives who have predeceased us—

our grandmother and mother Maniaten,

Shan Shushep,

Nishapet,

our grandfather and father Matshiu Ben.

and for Tanien Ashini,

my friend and cousin,

who passed away as I was writing this.

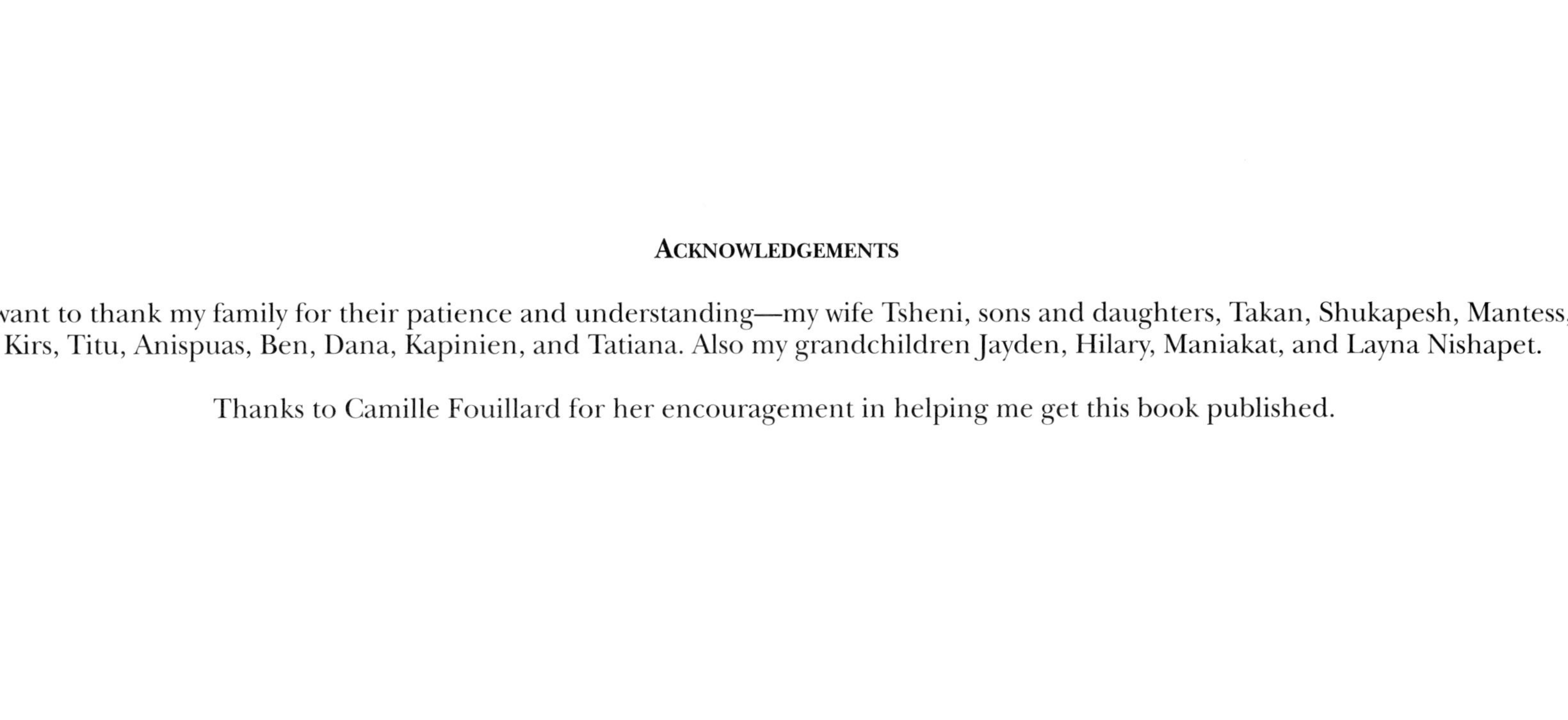

Acknowledgements

I want to thank my family for their patience and understanding—my wife Tsheni, sons and daughters, Takan, Shukapesh, Mantess, Kirs, Titu, Anispuas, Ben, Dana, Kapinien, and Tatiana. Also my grandchildren Jayden, Hilary, Maniakat, and Layna Nishapet.

Thanks to Camille Fouillard for her encouragement in helping me get this book published.

If I could write, I would write you a story...

– Maniaten Antane

These words are my mother's words and why this book was born. Her words have persisted long after she passed away and returned to the home of our ancestors. She often told stories about her life and struggles both in the country and in Sheshatshiu. My concern was that her words would forever be lost if they were not written down. I want to save her stories so that our future family can read and forever cherish the lives of our people who despaired but triumphed despite their struggles. I want all our family to love and respect my mother as the leader, mother, grandmother, and mentor she was to all her children. Her story is Giant's story too...

– Nikashant Antane

Foreword

This book tells the story of the tenacity and courage of Giant (Michel) Andrew, a young, troubled Innu man, as he snowshoed for five weeks in 2009 through the backwoods of northeastern Labrador from Sheshatshiu to Natuashish to raise money and awareness to help beat diabetes. As the story of his journey unfolds, another story is also told—that of the tenacity and resilience of Giant's ancestors and all Innu as they struggled to find their way through a rapidly changing cultural landscape and the aggressive encroachment of Euro-Canadian society during the last century.

The Innu are a people who inhabit Nitassinan, the Innu word for "Our Homeland," which encompasses a large portion of the Quebec-Labrador peninsula. Nitassinan is a vast area of boreal forest, lakes, rivers, and barrens. Archaeological evidence indicates the Innu have inhabited Nitassinan for thousands of years.

Until recently the Innu were known as the Montagnais and Naskapi people. Today they number about 25,000. The majority live in 11 communities in Quebec, mostly along the North Shore of the St. Lawrence River. About 2,350 live in two communities in Labrador, in Sheshatshiu, where Kakatshu-utshishtun (Grand Lake) meets Atatshuinipek^{u} (Lake Melville), and in Natuashish, 300 kilometres to the north on the coast of Labrador. Sheshatshiu is home to 1,500 Innu and Natuashish to 850.

Before settlement became a way of life during the latter half of the last century, the Labrador Innu lived a nomadic life for most of the year when waterways were frozen and the land covered with snow. Small groups of two or three families would journey to the interior in search of game, walking on snowshoes and pulling their possessions on toboggans. In the summer they traveled by birch bark canoe to various gathering places, including Kauishatukuants (Old Davis Inlet), North West River (across the river from Sheshatshiu) and Uashat (Sept Iles). Here they traded, arranged marriages, and held feasts and other celebrations. They lived off the bounty of the land, hunting small mammals and waterfowl, fishing and gathering berries. At the heart of their culture was the caribou that migrated across Nitassinan in the spring and fall. The caribou provided them with food, as well as clothing, shelter and tools. Innu technology was well adapted to their environment. They were experts at making skin clothing, snowshoes, toboggans and canoes, as well as tools, weapons and utensils out of wood, stone and bone. They practiced their own medicine. Their diet was very rich in meats, with few carbohydrates.

The traditional world of the Innu was filled with spirits, related to animals and forces of nature. Spiritual practices were integrated into everyday activities. Rituals and feasts were held in conjunction with all hunting activities. Shamans communicated with the Animal Masters to foretell future hunting, but each hunter could obtain spiritual power through dreams, songs and by performing rituals of respect for all Animal Masters. Innu spirituality stressed egalitarianism. Humans were seen as equal and integral to nature, as opposed to superior. The hunt was not a conquest. If the hunter showed respect to the Animal Master, the animal gave itself up willingly. After a successful caribou hunt, a mukuashan (feast of the caribou) was held to honor the spirit of the caribou.

Giant (Michel) Andrew

The arrival in the 1800s of European trading posts in Nitassinan, and subsequent attempts to get Innu to trap furs to trade rather than hunt for subsistence, began an era of change. While the Innu became dependent on trading for food and supplies, they also ran into increasing competition with white and settler fur trappers. The collapse of fur prices in the 1930s and a reduction in caribou numbers caused great hardship, including starvation. The Innu began showing up at trading posts on the coast in a desperate condition, seeking assistance from missionaries, traders, and the government. They were also beset by illness and death from European diseases.

In the 1950s the government of Newfoundland and Labrador decided it was time to settle the Labrador Innu and began to construct houses for them in Sheshasthiu and later in the 1960s in Utshimassits (Davis Inlet). The government also began to provide social assistance and enforce wildlife hunting regulations. Schools were opened in the 1960s, taking children away from the hunting way of life. The need to send children to school made it necessary for parents to stay close to the village, but living in a settlement meant adults could not make a living hunting and trapping.

Settlement coincided with a number of industrial developments on Innu territory, including the mines at Labrador City, Wabush and Schefferville, and the flooding of the Smallwood Reservoir for the Churchill Falls hydroelectric project. Forestry projects and road developments resulted in a further incursion into Innu land.

Colonization—the process of subjecting the Innu to foreign institutions such as courts, education, the church, and governments, and opening their territory to a multitude of developments—deprived them of control over their lives. A once active, proud and independent people became cut off from their culture. Life in the village turned out to be one of squalor, family breakdown, violence, drunkenness, suicide, accidents, malnutrition, and illness, including diabetes.

But the Innu never fully surrendered to this process of assimilation. They continued to return to the land. In the 1970s when government introduced band councils in the two communities, the councils quickly implemented outpost programs to finance the cost of chartering planes to hunting camps in the interior of Nitassinan each spring and fall. Whole families embarked on sojourns of up to three months to return to their way of life and ensure that their children would learn Innu practices, skills, language, values, and beliefs.

A once active, proud and independent people became cut off from their culture.

In the late 1980s the Innu decided they needed to fight back and wrest control of their lives and their land. They organized a series of spectacular acts of disobedience—actions that continued into the 1990s and forced the provincial and national governments to pay attention more than once. The first protest occurred in 1987, when a group of Innu hunters, women, children and elders headed for Akamiuapishk^{u} (the Mealy Mountains) to shoot caribou where their ancestors had always shot caribou, but where the Newfoundland government insisted hunting was illegal. Women and children sat on the caribou to prevent the wildlife officers from confiscating them as evidence. In court, the Innu had no defense and entered no plea. Instead they read out a statement that said, “We believe deeply that this foreign law is not our law, and the right claimed by others to govern us and dispose of our lands and resources is not legitimate.” While some of the hunters were jailed, the Innu saw the action as a victory, one that had brought them together and made them stronger and worthy of respect.

The following year, Canada decided to invite its European allies to set up a NATO superbase, to conduct up to 40,000 military test flights and to practice aerial combat and bombings on Innu land. For years the Innu had already been the brunt of 6,500 low-level test flights at speeds of up to 900 kilometres an hour and as low as 30 metres above the ground. The noise of the killer planes startled hunters, terrified children, frightened the animals and polluted the waterways. The Innu decided to confront NATO’s military might head on. Hundreds camped on the grounds of the air base at Goose Bay. On more than 15 occasions, they marched onto the runways to halt the killer jets before take-off. Repeatedly, they also invaded the forbidden bombing range near Minei-nipi (Burbot Lake). Through their actions, they attracted worldwide attention. Plans for the NATO base were cancelled and the federal government was forced to put the Innu on the shortlist for land-rights negotiations.

Home!

During this time the Innu also began to demand control of their schools, as well as health and social services. This devolution process occurred over the last two decades, and in 2011 both Sheshatshiu and Natuashish now operate their own medical clinics, social health programs, and schools. Many Innu are also involved in a variety of businesses.

Innu leaders are on the verge of finalizing a 600-page land rights agreement that provides the Innu with 34,000 square kilometres of land, $2 million per year in compensation for the flooding caused by Churchill Falls hydroelectric dam, a royalty regime for the Lower Churchill hydro development, and established economic areas where Innu are assured participation in resource projects. The agreement must first be ratified by the two communities. Although most Innu are likely to vote in favour of the agreement, many remain unconvinced that a land rights agreement and financial compensation will bring justice or solve their problems.

In the meantime, the Innu continue to live in a constant state of flux and conflict. Caught between two worlds, many struggle to find a balance between Innu and Euro-Canadian values and beliefs on a daily basis. The culture of waged work keeps ever increasing numbers of people tied to the community. More people recognize the need of formal education to succeed in their new reality. Other influences such as the mass media and new technologies also lure them to spend more time in the village.

On the other hand, many continue to try to spend time on the land and participate in the outpost program. As well, over the last few years a number of backwoods snowshoe treks and canoe trips have been organized, involving elders and youth. Reclaiming ancestral means of travel and reconnecting with traditional travel ways affirms that the Innu culture continues to be passed on from one generation to the next.

Giant Antane's 2009 Walk was one such walk to promote the Innu culture. He set out to raise awareness and money to beat diabetes, and to demonstrate by example that the Innu way of life is healing and healthy. Diabetes has become a disabling and deadly disease for the Innu and other First Nations in Canada. Type 2 Diabetes, a preventable chronic disease, is on the rise as people live increasingly inactive, high-stress lives and rely on processed convenience foods for most of their nutrition. The Innu of Sheshatshiu suffer from diabetes at an epidemic rate of 6 times the national average.

The Innu of Sheshatshiu suffer from diabetes at an epidemic rate of 6 times the national average.

Giant's dream to demonstrate that the path to good health is the Innu way of life is supported by a growing literature that documents how the most resilient First Nations communities are those where the culture is strong, where youth learn a sense of pride and identity, where traditional family values thrive, and where a connection with the land and its bounty perseveres.

In this book readers will accompany Giant on his journey through Nikashant Antane's powerful words and beautiful photographs. They will come to understand why so many, young and old both within and outside of Nitassinan, fell in love with Giant for the courage and hope he inspired through his expansive dream, frostbitten good looks, humble nature, and magnetic strength.

Camille Fouillard

A note about Innu names:

In this book the author Nikashant Antane has chosen to use the Innu names of the people in his story. Alex Andrew is Nikashant's Christian name. Most Innu have both an Innu name and an English or French Christian name. Innu names are often versions of the Christian name, but some are old names passed down through families. Many Innu are best known by their nicknames, which are usually in Innu but occasionally — as in Giant's case — in English.

Similarly Nikashant has used Innu place names in the book. In this case, Nikashant has chosen to include the corresponding English name in brackets, following the Innu name. Where this does not occur, it is because there is no English version of the Innu place name.

TABLE OF CONTENTS

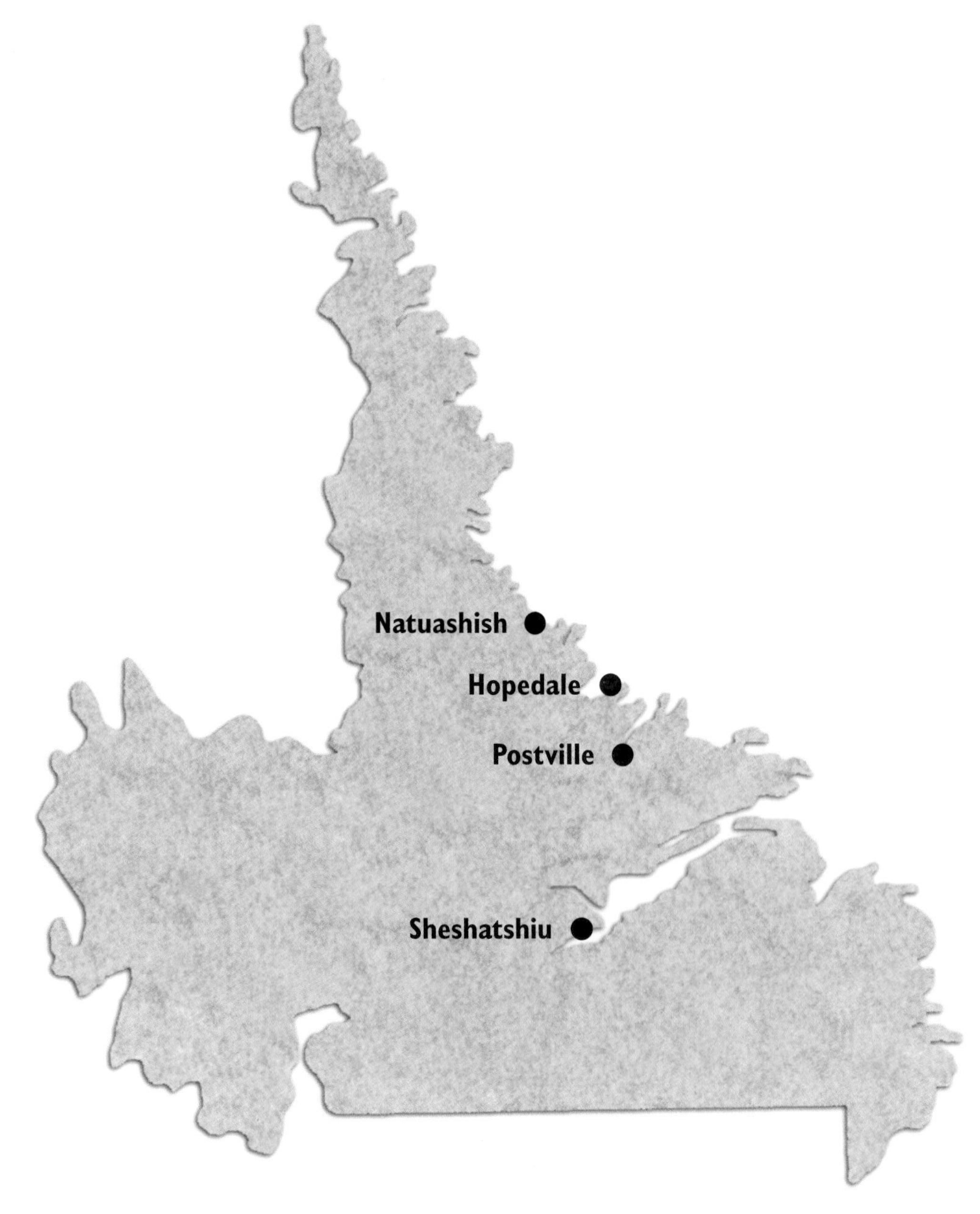
Natuashish
Hopedale
Postville
Sheshatshiu

Departure

On the way back from hunting ptarmigan on the Churchill Road one cold February evening, Giant turns to his uncle Nikashant in the truck.

"I had a dream that seemed so real last night," Giant says. "This old man told me to get up and help out the people. He said I should walk from Sheshatshiu to Natuashish to help people who have diabetes, like my uncle. So many people have diabetes. Look at all the people who've died from it, important leaders like Kauitenitakusht and Iskhuess died from complications of diabetes. In my dream I'm walking to Natuashish."

"That's a very long walk," Nikashant replies.

"There was zero diabetes among our people before. A walk like this would show people they need to get off their butt. The elders keep saying there's so much diabetes because people aren't active or eating the country foods we used to eat."

"You're really thinking about doing that walk?"

"I am. I want to set out in five or six days."

Nikashant Antane and Giant Antane. *Photo by Anthony Jenkinson*

"It's a good idea, but you don't want to rush into it. It'll take a lot of careful planning. Maybe you should plan for next year."

"Next year's not an option. I want to go soon. My grandfather never would've said he'd wait until next year to walk. He had to do it for survival. I wanna leave in a few days. Will you help me out a little?"

Nikashant sees that Giant is adamant. "Okay," he says to his nephew after a pause. "I'll help, but you have to tell your girlfriend first. You're supposed to go to St. John's with her to meet her parents. Maybe she'll blame me for doing this walk now."

"I'll tell Kat tonight."

"You should."

"I love that girl."

Nikashant says nothing. "Yeah, everybody gets that feeling once or twice in his life," he thinks to himself.

The two drive on in silence. Nikashant has observed how Giant and this Katherine Piercey have become inseparable. This new found girlfriend from Newfoundland seems to be helping Giant straighten out his life. For years now Giant has been a heavy drinker and doing drugs when he was not in *nutshimit* (the country). Nikashant saw his nephew's life spiral downward. He knows that Kat is good for Giant, but he wonders what would happen if she ever decided to break up with him. "Will I have to worry about this boy's life again?" His mind fills with all kinds of questions. "Would Giant go back to doing all that stuff?"

Meanwhile Giant's thoughts are on the man in his dream. He wonders who this elder could be.

"Do you have a picture of your father — my grandfather?" Giant asks, breaking the silence. Nikashant pulls up to Giant's house to drop him off for the night. "I have one on my computer. Come to my house tomorrow and I'll show it to you."

Matshiu Ben Antane

The following evening, Giant pays Nikashant a visit. The two head downstairs. Nikashant turns on his computer to show his nephew his grandfather's photo. The old computer turns and churns as it boots up. Nikashant opens his pictures folder, then goes to the top left hand corner and clicks on the icon of a lone figure. The faded photograph appears and he enlarges it.

"That's my grandfather?" Giant asks.

"That's him, Matshiu Ben Antane. He died of a heart attack four years before you were born."

"He's the old man in my dream." Giant continues to stare at the picture. "Nikashant, I really do have to go on this walk."

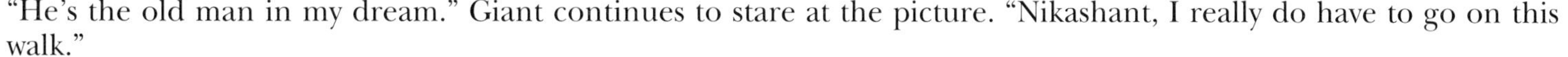

Giant leaves and Nikashant heads for bed, his mind racing with details. How should he start and who will he talk to first? Can Giant really do this walk all by himself? Nikashant knows he couldn't himself. He thinks about how Giant is really living up to his name – about the giant feat he has set out to accomplish. His deceased brother Shan Shushep (Charlie) would be so proud of Giant. He was the one who gave Giant his name. "You're not a baby. You're a Giant," he said many times, and the family began to call the boy Giant instead of his Christian name Michel. The nickname stuck.

The clear, starry night is cold as Giant walks briskly home. He thinks about what his uncle Aputet is always saying about Innu spirituality, about how the best hunter in an Innu family always takes care of his own whether he is still living or not. Giant knows his grandfather has moved back into the country, the place that was his home. He knows the man in his dream, the man in the photograph, will keep a close eye on him.

On February 11, 2009, six days after his dream, Giant packs up his gear in the small basement of his grandmother's home in Sheshatshiu. He wants to keep his load as light as possible. He packs a two-man tent made by an elder Kanani. He also piles on a small stove, an ax, a bucksaw, and rations of food. He notices he has too many small packs filled with food from well-wishers, several from people with diabetes. "I can't take all these," he thinks. "I wanted to be on my way by 7:00 and I'm still here packing my stuff." He doesn't realize that already, before he has even left, many people are inspired by his dream.

As he finishes packing, Kanani hurries in and tells Giant to put on a pair of pants she has just sewn. The pants match the Innu coat she'd stitched and delivered the night before. "It'll look better if you have matching pants," she says to him. The clothing is made of canvas and decorated with ribbon and bric-a-brac. Innu have long worn hunting jackets. At one time the coats were made of caribou hide. With natural dyes, women painted elaborate designs that were believed to empower the hunter.

Giant's aunt Mani Mat and great-aunt Tashtu
pray for Giant's safety as he embarks on his journey.

Giant pulls on the pants and finally rushes out the door. This point of departure is symbolic because it is the home where his grandmother raised him from the time he was a toddler. Although she is no longer around, he knows her spirit is out there with the crowd to bid him farewell.

Hundreds of people have come to see him off. The crowd—elders, Innu and non-Innu friends and well-wishers, the media and amateur photographers—stands in the cold, nippy morning air. Children, including his daughter Katienna, look on from two school buses.

"Hurry! It's cold," his biological mother Shustin says. "The elders want to say a prayer before you go." As Giant ties the last bit of gear onto his toboggan, his grandmother's sister Tashstu starts off the prayer and others follow along. When the prayer ends, Giant hugs Tashstu. "We know you can do it," she says. "I've seen you in the country. You are a hard worker." Giant hugs each elder, as they send him off with their blessings. "We will always be praying for you."

His girlfriend Kat moves from the silence and walks down from the snowbank along the road's edge to where Giant stands on the ice. They whisper a few words to each other. They kiss and hug.

Kat Piercey, Giant's girlfriend.

Children watch from school buses as Giant prepares to leave.

Many people hold back tears, but emotions erupt as he leaves. He waves one last time and heads out across the wide, empty ice of Atatshuinapek[u] (Lake Melville) toward his journey of healing and his battle against diabetes that has claimed so many of his people.

His cousin Ben hollers, "Don't give up Giant. We're with you."

His family watches as he walks into the horizon across the vast expanse of Atatshuinapek[u]. They hope he will be able to reach his destination — that he will find the stamina to climb the many hills, cut through the frozen bogs and continue the long way around bays to fulfill his dream.

Giant says his goodbyes. He holds onto his mother Shushtin the longest. Their eyes brim with tears. "*Nikau* (Mom)," he says. "I'll be okay. I know my grandfather's looking out for me and I'll make it. I want to help the people." He realizes this is the first time he has called her *Nikau.* He has never used this word with her. She did not raise him because their little family had broken up. She felt she had to give Giant up, her first son, to her mother when he was very young. It was his grandmother Maniaten he had always called *Nikau.* Today Shushtin reclaims her place.

"Another thing," Giant says to his mother. "I know my aunt Nishapet is really sick with terminal cancer. If she dies, I'll keep walking. I know that's what she wants. You tell her I'll always be thinking of her."

Friends and supporters are silent on the ice as they watch him adjust his gear stacked onto his toboggan. His girlfriend Kat moves from the silence and walks down from the snowbank along the road's edge to where Giant stands on the ice. They whisper a few words to each other. They kiss and hug.

Giant's mother Shustin says goodbye to Giant.

On His Own

Giant disappears into the wild country — a land often crisscrossed by his grandparents and their parents before them. As he snowshoes past Mokami Hill, towards Maunat (Mulligan), he thinks of his ancestors, how since time immemorial the Innu snow-shoed across Nitassinan (Innu homeland) towing their belongings on handmade toboggans. Their days revolved around a nomadic way of life. They struggled and persevered to survive. They depended on caribou for sustenance. In the spring, summer and fall, they traveled by canoe. Followers of the caribou, they journeyed regularly to caribou crossings on the Mushuau Shipu (George River) and other places throughout their land, like Meshikamau, Meneiku (Menihek), and Ashuanipi. Many Innu families would meet at these crossings and wait to spear the caribou as they reached the shore.

Giant finds it hard to believe that his grandparents could travel so far and wide by canoe and over numerous portages, and then across frozen barrens once winter settled in. His grandmother Maniaten shared many fond memories of these travels with him. She told him how each year they spent only a month in coastal gathering places and then moved back into *nutshimit* (the country) to look for the animals upon which they survived. He knows the story of how one time as a young child she was left in a camp with her mother and another family so that her father Shimun and another hunter could fetch supplies at Uashkaikan (Fort Chimo).

Another time Maniaten's family had set up camp deep inland looking for caribou when spring came early. "We don't have time to make it back to Uashat (Sept Isles)," Shimun told his wife and children. "We'll have to go to Utshimassits (Davis Inlet)." They traveled to the north coast and stayed with *Mushuau-Innu* (Innu of the Barrens) families. The Elders shared their stories and hunters shared their kill. During this sojourn, Shimun was fond of casting his net off a point near Utshimassits. Elders there came to call this point Shimun Kapatshatauat (Where Simon Cast His Net).

Maniaten told Giant about the many portages along their travels, and one in particular that was steep and long—the Kakatshat Pakatan along the Mishta Shipu (Moisie River). She talked about how she often heard people say that "Indians are lazy." But she would say, "I never knew this word lazy when I was growing up. If these people could travel with the Innu on one of their journeys, they'd change their assumptions right quick."

These were times when the wait for the caribou could be long, and people and children actually starved. The Innu had high regard for the *Mishtapeut* (Animal Masters). During times of hardship, they would contemplate whether it was a punishment of the *Mishtapeut* to keep the caribou away from their usual haunts. The *Kamanitushit* (Shaman) practiced rituals to determine why the caribou were not traveling through Innu hunting areas. In the *Kushapatshikan* (shaking tent), the *Kamanitushit* communicated with the *Mishtapeut* to see if the caribou were close or far away. Giant loved to hear Maniaten describe the time an Elder Shinapesht (Sylvester Antuan) performed a shaking tent. Shinapesht told the people to sit around the tent and be quiet. The old man entered the tent and although he had no drum, the people soon heard the beat of a drum beckoning the *Mishtapeut*, who responded one by one. The goose called out and thumped onto the ground as it landed in the tent. In turn as each animal entered the tent, the people heard its call and the thump of its landing. The rigid poles of the tent shook fiercely from the powers of the *Mishtapeut*. Maniaten spoke of the *Kushapatshikan* as the most beautiful experience of her life.

There are many stories Elders have passed on for generations—stories that taught Giant about the utmost respect the Innu are required to show all animals.

As Giant walks on his first day, one snowshoe step in front of the other, his mind often wanders to one or another of his grandmother's stories. Like what she taught him about the *Kanipanikassiut* (Caribou Master). He knows he will not be able to hunt caribou on this journey. The load would be too great to carry and Innu teachings say he must not waste any part of the animal. Each part of the caribou has a use and he must show respect for the *Kanipanikassiut.* On this journey he will only hunt small game to feed himself.

He trudges on across the vast icescape and thinks about how his grandmother used to say that the cod around Newfoundland were disappearing because Newfoundlanders lack respect. When Maniaten heard about the screech-in ceremonies performed by Newfoundlanders on visitors to their Island, she said this was why Newfoundlanders were losing their cod. During this ceremony the visitor becomes an honorary Newfoundlander by wearing a floppy fisherman's hat, swigging back a drink of rum, and kissing a dead codfish. Maniaten said people were making fun of the cod and the *Mistnaku* (Master of the Water Dwellers) would eventually punish them and make the fish less abundant. She knew from experience that it was always hard for the Innu when the *Mishtapeut* (Animal Masters) were angry with them. They could die from starvation if someone showed disrespect towards an animal.

As the first evening sets in, Giant's thoughts are on where he will spend the night. He is a little apprehensive about his first night in the wilds, a little scared of spending it all alone. But after his long day's trek, he meets up with a friend Richard Michelin who invites him to spend the night at his cabin at Sapashkuashua. The cabin is cozy and they eat partridge and caribou. Giant is pleased with his first day. He is bone-weary, but knows he will get stronger with each day. As he nods off to sleep, he does not know that his story is being told on the Newfoundland regional news.

The following morning he is off again after making minor adjustments to the load on his toboggan. The weather is cold but clear, perfect for traveling. He plods on steady all day and stops to set up camp at the base of a hill. He picks a spot sheltered from the cold northwesterlies that bring blizzards, and where there are plenty of young trees and firewood nearby. He removes his snowshoes to stomp down an area with his feet, where he will erect his tent. Then he puts his snowshoes back on and further packs down the tent's floor area until it is deep enough that the winds will not seep through. He chops down a number of small trees, shaves the branches off with his axe, and lays a thick cover of the boughs across the floor space. Using the tree trunks as tent poles, he digs them into the deep snow around the floor area forming a rectangle of poles to support the canvas tent. He fetches a nice long dry tree to use for the ridge pole across the top, and shaves it smooth to remove any splinters that could tear up the tent. He ties the ridge pole to a couple of support poles on either side of the tent, then stretches out each corner of the tent and ties them on. He packs snow around the tent for insulation, and sets up the small sheet metal stove and pipes just inside the tent, just to the right of the door. Splinters fly as he chops and splits a pile of firewood.

He fills the stove with chunks and just as he lies back warm and toasty in his tent, four hunters arrive to drop off some fresh ptarmigan that he fries up for his supper. The freezing night air breaks his sleep throughout the night. He must keep stuffing wood into his small homemade stove to keep the tent warm. He falls asleep quickly in the warmth, only to be awakened again within a few hours by the crisp cold.

As Giant walks these first couple of days, many friends call his uncle Nikashant, who has taken over the public relations work. Giant's girlfriend Kat helps out, as does a dietician Annette Stapenhorst, who works at the Innu health clinic. The phone calls trickle in at first, but by the end of the week many strangers are calling to contribute to the battle against diabetes.

Giant's friend Luke calls. "I was crying when I saw my friend leave and I feel so proud of him," he says to Nikashant, as he chokes up again. "Giant has awakened me. I'm glad he's gotten over his drinking."

He must keep stuffing wood into his small homemade stove to keep the tent warm.

Kat starts up a Facebook page, dedicated to her boyfriend's walk. In less than four days, hundreds of people have signed up and are posting inspiring comments. The comments start from Sheshatshiu and soon are pouring in from as far away as Argentina in South America. What started as a dream—to find the cure for diabetes—is now inspiring thousands of people to keep hope ticking ever stronger.

As Giant pulls his toboggan all alone in the country and each snowshoe scrunches into the snow, he does not realize that many people want to shake hands with the young man who is trying to make a difference. He is thinking, "I don't need recognition, I just want to help ordinary people battling diabetes." Every so often he stops, listens to his heartbeat like the beat of a drum played by an old man. He takes a breath and smiles as he moves on. He knows that his grandparents, Maniaten and Matshiu Ben, are following him on his journey.

Giant's grandfather Matshiu Ben was a young, vibrant and skilled hunter—a hard worker much like his grandson. Matshiu Ben was known as a trail maker. In times of heavy snow, he was the one to go ahead and break the trail for those who traveled with him.

As a young boy, Matshiu Ben traveled many a mile along with his parents and siblings, following their ancestors' footsteps. On one of their many journeys, they were canoeing by Kakuetipapukunanut on the Ashuanipi Shipu (Ashuanipi River), a place where canoes often overturned. Matshiu Ben sat at the centre of the canoe with his three-year-old brother perched on the *atshukuminsh* — a bundle of their belongings that was shaped like a seal. Matshiu Ben was content because they did not have to walk along the shore. All of a sudden he realized he was in the water gasping for air and reaching out for anything to hang onto. He desperately grabbed on to the *atshukuminsh* and was carried downstream in the raging river. Fortunately, families were following not far behind and someone hauled him out of the river.

His parents also survived the ordeal, but they soon realized that the youngest son was nowhere in sight. There was a frantic search but he was never found. This was a devastating and heartbreaking loss for Matshiu Ben because he had only one brother. Over the years whenever his mother Manishish talked about the ordeal she could never finish the story. She would start crying halfway through the telling. She always said that if the boy hadn't worn homemade suspenders, he might not have been caught underwater and would have survived.

As Matshiu Ben grew, Manishish was particularly proud of her young adult son because of his hard work helping others out. If anyone was ever in need when supplies ran short in their camp hundreds of miles from the nearest post, Matshiu Ben would often be the one to fetch more. He would be sent off alone. Manishish would say he always traveled faster alone and he preferred it that way. He had probably inherited spiritual powers from a distant relative Mashskuatuiapeu, who was a *Kamantushit* (Shaman). Stories are told that when Matshiu Ben traveled alone over snow, his snowshoes barely skimmed the surface. He traveled so fast that in less than a week he could fetch supplies from hundreds of miles away—a trip that would have taken others fourteen or fifteen days.

Matshiu Ben was very respectful of the animals he killed for food. He always hung the bones of the animals up in the trees. And he would return the bones of *Mistanku* (Water Dwellers), such as beavers and otters, back into the water. This is why his hunts were always successful. The *Mishtapeut* (Animal Masters) were content with him.

Many years later Matshiu Ben married his first wife Helen Ashini, the daughter of Shuashem and Anpinamen Ashini. They had six children. Their firstborn was Manikatnen (Mary Kathleen Nuna), who is still living at sixty-nine years of age. All the other siblings— Shan Shushep, Benuen, Etuet, Shushep and Manimatinen—died of pneumonia at a very young age. Tuberculosis was prevalent back in the thirties and forties, and Matshiu Ben's wife eventually succumbed to it. Many other Innu were treated out in Newfoundland, sometimes spending months and years away from their families.

With each day, Giant slowly feels stronger and healthier. His mind is clear, his body alive. He is reminded about how healthy this way of life is as he moves and breathes fresh air, away from all the stresses of community life. He thinks about how healthy his ancestors were before diseases like tuberculosis and diabetes were introduced to the Innu. Tuberculosis was once the dreaded disease, but now diabetes is ravaging his people. His uncle Aputet is struggling with diabetes because of too many years of being inactive and not eating country foods.

On this third day, Giant sets off again. He pulls the harness of his load across the front of his shoulders and yanks his body forward. He struggles to pull his heavy gear over steep hills, only to get to the top and see more hills beyond. He scours the terrain to find an easier route. He tries to walk over lake ice and frozen bogs as much as possible, but inevitably he must cut across more hills. He battles with his toboggan. It is too narrow and keeps tipping over, slowing him down. He kicks and curses it. Sometimes the snow is so deep, he must leave his toboggan and go ahead to break trail. His legs and back muscles ache as he trudges on. He pants, but can only stop for short intervals to catch his breath. He needs to move constantly because his sweat turns cold very quickly. He cannot pause until he is ready to build a large fire for a boil-up or in the stove as soon as the tent is erect. In a few more days, he knows he will feel better.

That night, he sets up camp by a stand of juniper trees. Once again, he pitches his tent with care so it will not be drafty. As the severe evening cold sets in, the trees crackle and split. Giant is awakened by a strange noise, like a thousand people screaming in the dark. Alarmed, he jumps up and frantically searches for his flashlight. He crawls out of the tent to discover that the noise is only the juniper trees screaming in the cold. He talks to his grandfather, whose presence he senses deep inside. He is consoled by the thought that his grandparents are with him. He looks up to see the night sky filled with stars and northern lights cackling from one end of the sky to the other. He knows tomorrow's weather will be cold and crisp and plans to get an early start.

The next morning he gets up and lights the stove. Through his canvas doorway, a small whiskey jack peers in and he throws it a small scrap of meat from the night before. The little bird snatches the gift and flies to a nearby juniper.

Giant does not linger. He quickly breaks camp. First he unties the support poles around the tent and shovels away the packed snow. He hauls out the stove and pipes, unties the ridge pole and slides it out. The tent falls to the ground. He folds it neatly, ties it up, and loads it onto his toboggan along with the stove and pipes.

As he sets out with his load trailing behind him, he says, "*Namushum* (Grandfather), please let this be another good walking day." With each day, he feels more confident and at ease, particularly now that he knows that the scream he heard during the night was only from trees swaying in the brittle cold.

The fifth day is a Sunday and Giant decides he needs a day of rest. His back aches from scaling hills and struggling through deep snow. He chops more wood, organizes his gear and hunts ptarmigan. The break does him good. The next morning he is keen to move on. He feels his legs growing stronger and he knows with each day he will be able to walk more kilometres than when he started off. Today the hills are easier to navigate. The weather is beautiful, sunny with blue skies, too warm to walk with a canvas jacket. When he stops for a boil-up, he chops wood in his t-shirt. Soon he is on his way again. Today as he snowshoes on, he thinks of his girlfriend Kat, how she has reinvigorated his life. He is filled with a great sense of healing that he has received from her. He wants to share the rest of his life with her. He tries to imagine how he might propose to her.

In Matshiu Ben's days, there were no marriage proposals. His marriage to Giant's grandmother Maniaten was arranged. Giant heard this story from her more than once. She told him about how her father and mother, Shimun and Manishish Gregoire, and their young children journeyed one time into *nutshimit* (the country) in two canoes from Uashat (Sept Isles). The two oldest teenage daughters, Manian and Maniaten, paddled one canoe with their many belongings. It took months of canoeing and portaging to get to their hunting area, a place called Meneiku (Menihek Lake).

After they had established themselves in their winter camp, Shimun discovered caribou nearby and decided to track them down. He set out the following morning and spotted the caribou in a circular esker out on the land. He killed many caribou with only a 22-calibre rifle. He returned to camp the next day with some of the meat. His wife and children were delighted and decided to move their camp to the sight of the kill. At the new camp, they began to prepare the meat. Shimun went out to find rocks to use to pound the meat after it had been hung to dry. The families made a lot of *neueikan* (dried meat). Once dried, the *neueiken* was crushed into a powder with the rocks.

The people also made plans for a *Mukuashan* (Feast of the Caribou). They crushed the end bones of the caribou legs and put the crushed bones into a pot of boiling water. Once the pot had cooled, the grease rose to the top. The marrow was placed in a bowl and the grease was poured on top, producing the *pimin* for the feast. The *pimin* was a sacred food. Every bit of it had to be eaten or used up in some way. Even the bits left on your fingers were used, like to rub it into a person's hair. The preparations were done. Shimun fetched other Innu nearby to share his kill. There was much to eat and the children were happy.

When it was time to go back to the coast for the summer, Shimun decided they should go to Sheshatshiu because his friend's father had gone there the previous year. Shimun also knew spring had arrived early and the ice would soon be breaking up. Uashat was too far to reach before break-up. The family headed to Meshikamau on the way to Sheshatshui where a number of Innu families had gathered. He asked one of the *utshimau* (leader of the hunt) for specific directions. The *utshimau* pointed him in the right direction and described the landscape over which he would travel. Later when Shimun told his wife and two teenaged daughters they would travel to Sheshatshiu, his wife said, "But you don't know where it is!"

"The elder has pointed me in the right direction," Shimun replied. "It's in my head now." The family parted ways with other Innu who had decided to stay year-round in Meshikamau.

Shimun followed the *utshimau*'s instructions and journeyed with his family until they came upon some snowshoe tracks. The next day Shimun set out alone to find out if there were people nearby. Sure enough, Shuashem and Anpinamen Ashini were camped a half day's walk away. At the time Giant's grandfather Matshiu Ben was living with his wife's parents Shuashem and Anpinamen even though she had died a while back.

The Ashinis greeted Shimun with warmth and fed him. They exchanged stories and Shimun learned that Sheshatshiu was only a day's walk away. The Ashinis decided to send Matshiu Ben with Shimun to help him out. The two set out. When they arrived at Shimun's camp, Matshiu Ben discovered a young girl he admired. He was looking at Maniaten. She was not interested because she had left her boyfriend behind in Uashat, but Matshiu Ben thought the two of them would make a good marriage. Before long Anpinamen visited Manishish Gregoire to say that Matshiu Ben should marry Maniaten. She did not have the option to turn it down because the practice in those days was to arrange the children's marriages. She did not love or even like Matshiu Ben, so she married him with great reluctance.

Matshiu Ben was quite content with his new, young wife. He named their oldest son Shan Shushep, the same name he had given his first son in his previous marriage. Matshiu Ben and Maniaten eventually had fifteen children, over sixty grandchildren, many more great grandchildren and some great, great grandchildren.

Maniaten always remembered her first boyfriend back in Uashat despite all the children she had with Matshiu Ben. She often mentioned her boyfriend to her children. One day, she told the story again, as she sat sipping tea in her kitchen with her daughters Puna and Shustin. Puna got mad. "Why are you always talking about this boyfriend?" she asked her mother. "How come you had fifteen children with my father if you didn't love him?"

"Shut up," Manieten said. "We never had birth control back then and you wouldn't be sitting here arguing with me today if we had." Puna just shut up. Shustin giggled at the outburst, but then as she gazed out the window, her thoughts wandered to her own troubled marriage.

Storm

Giant's mother Shustin is following her son's journey closely. Throughout each day she thinks of him constantly. She stares out of that same window from long ago and wonders how he is doing. She still agonizes about sending him off to live with his grandmother when he was barely out of diapers. As the years went on, she gave away three other sons and one daughter to be reared by relatives. She knew they would be safer away from her and their father. Now her children are grown. They are fond of their biological mother but they do not refer to her as Nikau. She is Shustin to them. Giant's walk has brought them closer. They all post good wishes for Giant on the Facebook site. They proudly read the full-page article about the walk in the local newspaper *The Labradorian.*

Shustin looks forward to traveling to Natuashish to await her son's arrival. She will be so proud of him when she sees him walk on the ice towards the hundreds of people who will await his arrival at the finish line. She dreams of how she will embrace the pride and joy she abandoned twenty-six years ago. She knows there won't be a dry eye amongst the crowd welcoming her first-ever son.

As the days pass Giant's uncle Nikashant continues to field calls from people at home and abroad who are concerned and want to know Giant's whereabouts. Giant is carrying a GPS spotter, a monitoring device that allows Nikashant to track his movements. Everyday Nikashant downloads a map produced with the GPS software so that anyone can track Giant's progress on the Facebook site. Some days when the walking is really good, Giant can cover thirty or forty kilometres. On other days the spotter indicates that Giant is still in the one place. Giant is also carrying a satellite phone that he uses to call only two people at two-day intervals—first his girlfriend Kat and then Nikashant. He reports that everything is okay and that he is getting stronger day by day.

Nearing the shores of Kapiokok Bay.

On February 20th, nine days into his walk, Giant senses a storm coming. The skies darken from the east. An experienced hunter, he always looks out for any changes in the weather. He does not take any chances because a blizzard could show up in a minute if he is not careful. He looks for a secure place to pitch his tent so that the cover of trees can lessen the blizzard's howling winds. Sure enough, a snowstorm starts to blow just as he finishes chopping firewood for the stove. But out here in *nutshimit* (the country), Giant is now at home.

Once settled in his tent, he cooks himself a feed of ptarmigan he hunted earlier that day. He fries the birds in a pan with butter and rice, adding flour and water to make gravy. He scrapes the final juices from the pan with bannock delivered yesterday by visitors from Sheshatshiu. After the meal, he lays back on his caribou bedding. Before sleep takes him, his thoughts wander as always to his grandparents. He thinks of all the places they traveled, of the lakes and rivers they crossed, highways of days gone by.

The Mishta Shipu (Churchill River) and Meshikamau Lake were one of the main travel ways for Giant's grandparents. In the 1960s when the Mishta Shipu was dammed for the Churchill Falls hydroelectric project, their lives changed dramatically. Waters near and far were affected. An endless number of dykes and dams flooded a vast territory, smothering an important travel system. Matshiu Ben would forever complain. Below the dam, the rivers were so shallow, the water barely went up to his knees. It hurt him gravely to see this travel route he had canoed so often diminished to a trickle in some places. A whole hunting and trapping area was lost and changed forever. The loss set in motion the transformation of a once proud hunting group into a diminished people dependent on government and their petty handouts.

While the hydroelectric project was being developed, governments and other authorities were busy exerting much pressure on the Innu to force them to give up their nomadic way of life. The church set up schools with the help of governments. Welfare and child allowance programs were introduced to persuade the Innu to settle into village life. Once the Innu were dependent on the new system, authorities threatened that if they took their children into *nutshimit* (the country), their family allowance would be cut.

Some Innu were intimidated by the threats and reluctantly abided by the rules. Other Innu insisted on living the ancestral way of life but soon discovered they faced other threats from foreigners. Once again established in their hunting areas, the Innu began to experience frequent flyovers from wildlife authorities to check on what they were hunting. If they killed caribou, wildlife officers raided the camp and charged them with illegal hunting. The Innu barely spoke English and did not understand why they were suddenly stopped from hunting the caribou that had sustained them for thousands of years. The wildlife officers were very aggressive and arrogant in their searches because the *akamakunuesht* (police) were at their side. The Innu, incensed by these violations, repeated the words of frustration *atumutakei* (dog's penis) and *atuminish* (monkey) to the authorities.

These were difficult times for Giant's grandfather Matshiu Ben. He was puzzled and felt humiliated. Without his knowledge and with no explanation, the government flooded his lands and took over his family. Matshiu Ben thought hard and long about the belongings he lost — canoes, traps, snowshoes, firearms. He mourned for all the graves along the Mishta Shipu, now lost forever beneath the flooding. He traveled to the area again, but the landscape was changed forever. Massive transmission lines were headed south and into another country. Greedy hydro companies were reaping profits by the millions. Each time people flicked on a switch in their massive offices and homes, they did not realize an injustice had been done to the homeland of the Innu.

Anthony Jenkinson photo

There are no electrical switches to flick in Giant's tent where he waits out the snowstorm that traps him one long day and then another. Stranded at his camp along the river a little ways from the mouth of Kapiokok Bay, he keeps stuffing wood into his stove to keep warm. He listens for weather reports on his hand-cranked radio. He also steps out of his tent to regularly check on the winds to see if they have changed around from the north to the west. At night he lights candles and studies the flicker of its flame across the canvas of the tent. On the second morning, he wakes to find his tent almost completely buried by the night's snowfall. The storm continues to swirl around him. He is stifled by the day's repetitive routine: getting wood, laying in wait, snacking, boiling up a cup of tea, watching the wind ripple and flap across the tent's canvas, staring at the fire through the small opening in the stove's door as the air gets sucked in and pushes the flames and smoke up through the pipes. Noises swoosh outside the tent from the relentless winds. Moments turn into hours, hours turn into days. The long wait begins to drain Giant's appetite to move forward with his dream. Does anyone care? Would anyone notice if he quit?

Meanwhile back home in Sheshatshiu, Giant's uncle Nikashant is swamped. His support work has become almost a full time effort, so he tells his superiors he needs two weeks off to continue coordinating Giant's campaign. Every day Nikashant fields an overwhelming number of calls from media and the public from every part of the world. Both his home phone and his cell ring steadily. He is constantly on the computer replying to all the e-mails of support.

Giant's girlfriend Kat is just as busy accepting contributions from people, companies, and organizations. She is also overwhelmed. Her co-workers kick-start the contributions by raising $315.00 selling snack foods during their dinner break. The children from the local school walk a few kilometres to show their support and the Charles J. Andrew Youth Treatment Centre raises funds for the cause. All the construction workers in the new housing project decide to each donate $50.00 from their next pay. The momentum mounts everywhere.

Nikashant is also in touch with the people of Postville. The community is getting excited and plans are underway for Giant's arrival. Brenda Colbourne, who works for the Health Department of the Nunatsiavut Government, volunteers to organize the event. As soon as she learns Giant will be passing through Postville, she starts looking for a contact person in Sheshatshiu. She phones Tenish Penashue's house and is given Nikashant's name. He gets the message and calls Brenda right away, hoping he can find a place for Giant to sleep in Postville.

A man picks up the phone and Nikashant asks for Brenda Colbourne. "I hope he doesn't get the wrong idea," Nikashant says to himself. Brenda takes the phone and Nikashant introduces himself as Giant's uncle. Brenda is ecstatic. They exchange phone numbers and e-mail addresses. Brenda says not to worry about where Giant will stay. The hotel manager has already offered up a free room for his stopover. Exchanges fly across cyberspace between Brenda and Nikashant about Giant's location and estimated time of arrival. The whole community of Postville is getting restless. A big banner has been made for him and a potluck supper is planned. The school children are also excited because they have planned their own celebration.

Nikashant has recruited his two friends to shadow Giant for the rest of his walk. Napess Ashini and his friend Anthony Jenkinson are experienced outdoorsmen and Nikashant knows they will enjoy the task. The plan is for them to drive ahead of Giant each day to break trail and set up camp for him at night. This will allow Giant to walk longer distances.

Bad weather delays the shadow team's departure. Finally after two days, they are delighted to hear from Nikashant that Giant will be on the move again the following morning. The two set out early on snowmobile, but all day the going is hard as they try to track down Giant. At one point they drive into a storm and are forced to turn back. The snow is too deep and they are running out of gas. Unbeknownst to them, they are only about five kilometres away from Giant's camp.

In the meantime Giant is far removed from this hub of activity and all the efforts being taken on his behalf. As another day of the storm stretches on, his frustration grows. The following morning, he heads out early before dawn although the weather is not great. As soon as he hits the first point, the winds pick up again and another blizzard blows in. After towing his toboggan for three kilometres, whiteout conditions force him to turn back. He knows it is not safe to continue. He quickly pitches his tent again and braces himself for another interminable day. As the day's hours drag on, he wonders what he is doing alone out in the middle of nowhere pursuing a foolish dream. The stories of his grandfather are his only company. He is reminded of how Matshiu Ben was not a man easily defeated by the injustices of an encroaching society.

One day an *akaneshau* (Whiteman) approached Matshiu Ben. The aspiring politican was accompanied by an Innu translator Shimun Michel who could barely speak English. The *akaneshau* asked Matshiu Ben if he wanted to live in a home with running water. Matshiu Ben said yes.

"Okay. Vote for this man come election time," Shimun told him. The *akaneshau*, with a big grin on his face, shook hands with Matshiu Ben. When the election rolled around he won, but Matshiu Ben never got to see his home with running water.

"Where's my running water?" Mathsiu Ben asked Shimun when he saw him many months later.

"Maybe he meant you'll get it next year," Shimun replied.

Matshiu Ben didn't wait around. He cut his own logs at the government sawmill to build a small two-bedroom home for his family in Sheshatshiu. He got pipes and a manual hand pump and dug a twelve-foot hole under his house. He installed the pipes underground and right through the floor of the house. Before too long, Matshiu Ben and his family were pumping their own water. Soon all his neighbours were getting water at his house. His well drew good, fresh water. He also helped some of his neighbours install their own wells.

From his house Matshiu Ben would set out to the mountains early in the mornings during winter to hunt caribou to feed his family. He walked on snowshoes and pulled a toboggan. He was proud to be able to feed his family just by going out on the land — something he had done his whole life. But his pride was short-lived.

He soon learned about restrictions being imposed on hunting caribou in the mountains. Now he felt a burden of animosity towards the society restricting the free life he knew best. The pressure was mounting. He felt deprived of his children because of his long absences. He continually argued with his wife. They fought over the constant threats from Social Services and the missionaries that they would lose their family allowance and social assistance if he took the children into the country for a long while. The argument centered around whether to send the children to school or not. Matshiu Ben wanted to bring them to *nutshimit* (the country) while Maniaten feared the loss of income from the government. She would tell Matshiu Ben to go to *nutshimit* by himself. Matshiu Ben tried that out. He hunted and trapped by himself but found it was not the same without his family.

In the village Matshiu Ben began to drink excessively to drive away thoughts of how the life he knew best was rapidly eroding. He saw his family moving towards a cursed life that was foreign to him. These thoughts were further aggravated when he saw his children going to school. "Why are my children learning the ways of another society and neglecting my traditional culture and way of life in *nutshimit*?" he often thought to himself.

School children walk to show their support for Giant.

Matshiu Ben never lived to see running water in his home. The *akaneshau* politician, who had promised him a house and running water, lost in the following election but continued to thrive in his business. This did not impress Matshiu Ben. His philosophy was, "Why make so much money when you can't take it with you when you die?" But his changing life was not so simple. Money woes haunted him the rest of his life as he continued to try to support his family and found himself torn between the two worlds of *nutshimit* and the community.

Giant is not so sure about being alone on this journey in *nutshimit* as the relentless snowstorm drives him to the edge. Day after day the storm blows on. He will surely go stir crazy faced with one more day. He lays back, stares at the ceiling and counts all the small holes in the canvas. The warmth of the stove and the crackling of the fire continually lull him to sleep throughout the day. One night as the storm continues its ferocious assault, a loud bang stirs him from his sleep. His stovepipes have come apart and are swaying wildly inside the tent. Flames shoot out of the stove. He leaps out of bed, grabs his mitts and manages to rehook the pipes before the fire ravages his tent. Giant falls back into a light sleep, unnerved by the storm's might.

In the morning the blizzard shows no sign of abetting. Restless and disgusted at not being able to move, Giant starts thinking it is time to call it quits. For almost two weeks he has walked, sometimes breaking his own trail for many kilometres in the deep snow, then having to backtrack to get his gear before he could move on to set up another camp before dusk. He is alone, feeling abandoned, with thoughts that nobody cares about what he is doing.

He thinks he will wait another day before he decides whether to continue, but that night when the storm still refuses to subside, he grabs his satellite phone. The phone rings at Nikashant's house around 9:00 p.m. and he picks up.

"I don't have too many minutes left on my phone," Giant says to his uncle. "But I need to tell you I'm quitting. Could you pick me up tomorrow?"

After a short pause, Nikashant says, "Are you sure?"

"The weather is really getting me down," Giant says. "I'm not used to just lying around. I can't stand it."

"Okay, I will get someone to pick you up once the weather clears."

"I'm about six hours away by snowmobile."

"Call me tomorrow and I will try to make some contacts tonight to find someone to do the pickup."

Static crackles on the phone line causing a pause in the conversation.

"Hey, the school kids were walking on the road yesterday to show the community's support for your walk," Nikashant adds.

This news shakes Giant. He is reminded that at least the students have noticed his walk and recognize his intentions to raise awareness about diabetes. He hangs up the phone. "No, I'm not giving up. I'm healthy and strong and people are struggling with the diabetes disease. I must help them," he thinks to himself.

The next morning before daybreak, he wakes up and lights the stove to warm up and drink a cup of hot tea before calling his uncle. Around 7:00 Nikashant hears his phone ring again.

"It's Giant. Don't bother about the pickup. I'm going to keep walking towards Postville as soon as I take down my tent."

Nikashant is so relieved. As soon as he puts down the phone, it rings again. Shamani, the local community radio broadcaster, is on the line. All night Nikashant wondered what he would say to Shamani when he made his daily call for the update on Giant.

"Hey, did I get you up? How's Giant?" John asks on air. "People are wondering where he's at now? So many people are calling the station with words of encouragement and hope."

"Phew, that was a close one," Nikashant thinks to himself. Over the radio waves, he says proudly, "Giant will in Kaipokok Bay today and should be in Postville hopefully tomorrow."

Again Nikashant fields calls all day from different Innu who want to talk about Giant and his walk.

"Me and my wife are so proud of this young man," Napess Riche says to Nikashant on the phone. "How could one person from our community be so inspiring and so strong fighting on behalf of diabetic people. Tell him how proud we are of him, will you?"

Meanwhile that morning, without thinking too much, Giant grabs a little grub and heads out to break trail in the deep snow. After walking many kilometres all morning, he turns back to return to his camp. His thoughts have lightened. He hears a snowmobile in the distance and is delighted to see his shadow team Napess and Anthony, who finally show up after heading out again from Sheshatshiu that morning. They arrive just as the wind has started to pick up again. Giant is eager to see them and very happy to receive their gifts of caribou meat, bannock, and raspberries—a small feast. The three sip tea and warm up in the tent.

"You walked a long way. We almost caught up to you last night, but we turned back because we were running out of gas," Napess said.

Anthony looks over at Giant, how he has lost so much weight and looks tired and thin from struggling such a long distance in the deep snow. He feels sorry for him, but says nothing. That night the three huddle together like sardines in Giant's small tent. Napess and Anthony share stories of how Giant has inspired so many people from his home province and abroad. This is just the boost Giant needs.

Finally their chatter slows down. Giant blows out the candle. He is excited about finally being able to continue his journey. The news that so many people are touched by his efforts strengthens his determination. He is feeling rejuvenated by the thought of the children who walked out of school to show their support for his cause. These children are learning a new story. New memories are being created for them. Giant thanks his grandparents' spirits for the strength they give him. "Give me another good day of walking tomorrow. Thanks for watching over me as I walk in your footsteps on our land."

"Give me another good day of walking tomorrow. Thanks for watching over me as I walk in your footsteps on our land."

As young children, Giant's grandparents knew only their culture and life on the land. It was a life intimately connected to the spirits of their ancestors, the animals and the world around them. They were raised with these beliefs, but once settled in the village, this spirituality began to fade. It no longer made sense. The Catholic Church, its lone God, and its Black Robe (the priest) were determined in their arrogance to replace the Innu world of spirits.

In Sheshatshiu Matsiu Ben and Maniaten were among the Innu who attended mass with their children. Men and women sat on opposite sides of the church. Matshiu Ben always found a seat near the back so he could partially sleep during the preaching. One day he sat quietly thinking about how the Black Robe was observing the congregation, taking note of who was absent from mass. He was sure to pay a visit to those people once the ceremony was over. A few people hung around after mass to wait and see who the Black Robe would haul back down to the rectory to repent and sometimes take a beating.

This was the same Black Robe who told a respected hunter—a practicing *Kamanitushit* (shaman)—that he was doing the work of the devil. This story hurt and angered Matshiu Ben. He knew for a fact that no Innu would be around today if it weren't for the people who practiced shamanism. They were the most accomplished hunters who communicated with the *Mishtapeut* (Animal Spirits).

One day the Black Robe announced that the Bishop was to visit in the near future and he wanted to see everyone at the service. Matshiu Ben planned to attend and told his children the Bishop was the only person holy enough to talk directly to God.

Maniaten attended mass during the week where she was reminded that the Bishop's arrival was fast approaching. She had only a couple of days to do all her laundry and make sure everyone looked their best. Now that they had the water pump installed by Matshiu Ben in their small home, they could pump water by hand for drinking and doing the laundry. Her daughters Manimat and Nishapet took turns pumping and carrying the heavy load to heat on the stove. All three had a hand at washing the clothes and hanging them on the line.

On that Sunday Maniaten's children and husband wore clean clothing to meet the Bishop. "If you kiss the ring of the Bishop, you'll all go to heaven," Maniaten told her family. There was excitement amongst the children. They all wanted to go to heaven. The family attended mass and as the service was ending, the Black Robe told the people and children to line up outside to kiss the Bishop's ring. Maniaten and Matshiu Ben fell in line with their children ahead of them so they could watch each one kneel and kiss the Bishop's big, blue, and holy ring. The Black Robe was very impressed that the Innu who were drinkers had abstained, so they could kiss the Bishop's ring. He could not read Matshiu Ben's thoughts, "Once the service is all over, I'll visit my cousin Alphonse to see if his homebrew's brewing right."

Later Matshiu Ben could be heard from quite far hollering his way home. Alphonse's homebrew must have been brewing right. Maniaten gathered all her children and told them to hide in the eldest son's room. They were to sleep on the floor. The eldest who was 16 was to keep his brothers and sisters safe. He was old enough to stop his father from fighting his mother. When Matshiu Ben came in through the door he did not holler, but in an angry voice he sang out every blasphemous word he knew as he danced around the cast iron wood stove. Maniaten told Mathsiu Ben to shush and stop swearing in front of the children.

"You kissed the holy ring today," she reminded him.

"I don't care," he replied. He mumbled that those people had taken away his land and deprived him of his children. He danced around the stove some more and chanted away. "Hai, hai, hai, hai, hai, hai." With all the thumping from his dance, the oven that sat on the stove fell to the ground.

Matshiu Ben finally stopped. He too was broken. He remembered the life when he was free out on the land. He fell asleep crouched over, sitting on his legs — the position in which he slept out in the bush when he only had an open fire.

The following day Matshiu Ben woke early and left the house and village behind. He walked far out on his land to Kamiuapishkut (Mealy Mountains). He hunted and honoured the *Mishtapeut* (Animal Masters), returned home with his kill, and his family welcomed him back. His dog barked as he reached the house and his children ran out to see the two caribou strapped onto his toboggan. Yesterday's tears of shame had evaporated. The proud hunter was panting from the heavy load and he asked for tea. He cached his kill on a nearby tree and entered the house.

Giant awakes to thoughts of his grandfather. He fires up the stove and boils up a kettle of water for his tea. Today he will try to make it to Kaipokok Bay, that has eluded him for so long. This is the place where his grandfather worked for twenty-two summers. Giant grabs a bite — leftovers from last night: some oats, berries, bannock and washes them down with his cup of tea. He breaks camp and heads out. It is a bright sunny day, but cold. As he walks twenty kilometres in heavy and drifting snow, he is looking forward to seeing his uncle Nikashant again.

Meanwhile Nikashant is traveling to Postville with other friends and family, including his wife Tsheni, Napess Riche, Kautu, Giant's mother Shustin, and Damien Castro, a family friend from Argentina. Their plane lands in the afternoon. They gather their luggage and head straight for the hotel, where the manager Carson Jacques greets them.

"Who's the Chief?" Carson asks.

"The Chief didn't make it today. She's planning to be in Natuashish when Giant gets there," Nikashant replies.

"That's okay. How about you be Chief and get the biggest room?"

"Let's go!" Nikashant says, laughing.

The first order of business is to find Brenda Colbourne, the local organizer for the walk. Nikashant is very happy to finally meet her and she quickly endears herself to the whole group. She scrounges up winter clothing to make sure they will be warm when they go meet up with Giant on snowmobile. The group grabs a bite to eat and bunks down early. They want to go find Giant first thing in the morning.

As the sun begins to sink into the horizon, Giant decides to set up camp in a wooded area, just a couple of kilometres south of Kapiokok Bay. He knows he could make it to Postville, but nightfall would beat him and he does not want to walk in the dark. Napess and Anthony help him set up camp, then carry on to spend the night in Postville.

The next morning Giant wakes up, yawns and stretches his limbs. Just as he is lighting the fire in his stove, he hears the sound of snowmobiles in the distance. Nikashant pulls up towing his Argentinian friend Damien Castro in a komatik box. Shushtin sits on the back of the snowmobile. Nikashant looks back to see Damien crouched deep into the box. He rushes over to check on him.

"What's wrong?" he asks.

"Freeze, freeze, freeze!" Damien sits up looking at his hands protected only with cotton gloves.

"Go warm up in the tent."

Giant greets Damien, takes his hands into his own, and rubs them vigorously. Before too long the colour returns to Damien's hands as the blood begins to circulate again. "Thanks," he says to Giant. Damien is a computer programmer who now works in the Department of Anthropology at the university in St. John's. In 2008 he spent six weeks in the country with the Antane family.

"Your friend is crazy," Giant says to Nikashant. "You can't be wearing cotton gloves in this weather. He must think he's back home in the Amazon." Giant gives him a proper pair of mitts.

Shustin, stands in the doorway of her son's small tent and looks over his things.

"Giant, you've come a long way," she says. "We followed your tracks."

"I'm only halfway there," he says. "But I'm finally going to make it to my first community. Postville, here I come!"

Everyone pitches in to break camp and Giant soon heaves off on his snowshoes, the weight of his toboggan jerking forward. His uncle and friends bolt back the ten kilometres to Postville. As they grab a quick lunch, Brenda walks in dressed in a traditional Inuit coat. She asks Shushtin if she would like to join a group of eight women walking to Big Point to greet Giant. Shustin agrees. The going is hard and she is the last to make it to Big Point. It has been too long since she walked on snowshoes. She thinks about how she should follow her son's example and get more active.

People from Makkovik are also traveling the southern edge of the Bay to meet up with the day's hero. Giant has bypassed Makkovik, so the travelers are coming to him to cheer him on. They are drawn by Giant's commitment to create awareness about diabetes and want to shake his hand and wish him well on his journey. That morning as news traveled the airwaves to let people know that Giant would hit Postville that day, Katie Winter begged her 82-year-old father Albert to drive her to Postville to meet Giant. She is diabetic herself and wanted to thank him personally for his efforts. Albert agreed to drive her and they traveled two freezing hours on snowmobile to Postville. Katie hung on tightly to the placard she made for Giant's welcome. They arrive as Postville puts the finishing touches on their preparations for the welcome celebrations.

Meanwhile Giant walks all morning. He stops for his usual lunch of *neueikan* (dried caribou meat), bannock, and a variety of dried fruits and nuts that he also snacks on throughout the day to fuel his body. The snow is packed hard, just the kind of snow that makes the going easy. He looks over to the east where the Kaikopok River empties into the Bay and thinks about his grandfather, how he spent many summers working in this area to scrounge up a bit of seasonal cash to support his family back home in Sheshatshiu.

Postville

Matshiu Ben, like other Innu, knew he had to make money. He felt cornered into this new lifestyle. In order for him to put food on the table, he had to work for cash or wait for petty government handouts. Eventually he chose to find work with an exploration company that was looking for guides and labourers. The Brinex Company was surveying for minerals, especially uranium, which was highly valued in the 1960s.

For twenty-two years, Matshiu Ben worked for Brinex from early June to late October. He began as a labourer and was eventually picked to work as a prospector alongside a Settler, with the surname of Michelin from North West River. Their job was to guide the geologists to potential mineral sites in the country.

Matshiu Ben walked long distances through the woods and bog looking for rock that moved the needle on his Geiger counter. On one of his trips, Mathsiu found a spot that looked promising. He took a sample of the rock, carried it back to his fellow prospector and told him where he had found it. The site is now called the Michelin deposit, a place name Matshiu Ben always disputed.

Matshiu Ben soon learned that his partner had received a $500.00 bonus for his find. Matshiu Ben got nothing. When he returned home, he talked to his wife and children about how he had found a rock that could be made into a nuclear bomb. He told them how his fellow worker had been paid a bonus. Distraught, he told his oldest son Shan Shushep (Charlie Andrew) to write to his boss. Shan Shushep wrote the letter and after a long wait, Matshiu Ben received a wood stove from the company.

Giant wonders where the Michelin deposit lies as he snowshoes from the mouth of the Kaipokok Bay along its southern shore. As he walks he looks far into the distance at the towering Post Hill, as it is known by locals. He is impressed by its size. He stops, scans the bay, and lights up a cigarette. He knows he needs to break this bad habit, but he very much enjoys the long draw of a cigarette when he stops to rest and drink tea. He has inherited the habit from his grandfather who always said, "I don't mind not eating, but I can't go without my tea and tobacco."

Giant moves on again and as his snowshoes crunch down one after the other onto the snowmobile trail, he spots a group of people waiting at Big Point. The group includes the Postville women and Shustin. Other supporters from Sheshatshiu and Postville have also joined them. When Giant finally reaches the group, he heads straight for his mother. He spreads his arms and gives her a great big bear hug.

"Now I'm actually more than halfway there," he tells her, as he gives her another big hug. Shustin fights back tears, remembering, wanting to say how sorry she is that she let him go as a child. A Postville man, Tommy, who Giant knew when they both worked at the Voisey's Bay mine, walks over to shake hands and congratulate him.

"I'll walk with you to Postville," Tommy tells his friend. A number of supporters follow behind.

"Are ya still working at Voisey's or whah?" Giant asks Tommy. The two talk about their time together at the Inco mine. Giant had made good money there, but always squandered it away whenever he got back home. He would land in Goose Bay and not even make it to Sheshatshiu. He invited

Giant poses with Albert and Katie Winter, who traveled from Makkovik to show their support.

his friends to come to the hotel and go on the booze with him. Later he would phone his uncle Nikashant. "Pick me up," he would say. "I'm done partying." Nikashant knew his nephew had problems and was always trying to talk him out of drinking.

But today Giant is heading for a different kind of party. The sun shines down on him, Tommy, and the women. The day is perfect for walking, just the right kind of cold. The group is dwarfed by the hills. Finally they are approaching Postville, which lies about 176 kilometres as the crow files northeast of Goose Bay. Post Hill overlooks the village. A crowd of about 150 people circles around Giant as he nears the village. The mayor offers greetings from the community and invites Giant to a supper at the school gym.

After the formalities, many come over to talk to Giant. Old Albert Winter and his daughter Katie from Makkovik stand at the edge of the crowd waiting to talk to him. Katie holds her placard still rolled up. When they get their chance to approach him, Albert tells him he drove with his diabetic daughter all the way from Makkovik to meet him. Katie proudly unveils the placard reading "Way to go, Giant!" Giant is so impressed he gives Katie a big hug and lets her hold his walking stick, which he refers to as his magic stick. "Come over and take a picture," he hollers over to Nikashant. "I want a picture with these guys." Others line up too and cameras snap photos, one after the other.

Giant grabs the rope from his tobbogan and tows it slowly into the community, following the snowmobile trail straight to the hotel. He goes to his room, turns up the heat, and grabs his first shower in weeks.

"I feel like a new man," he says to Nikashant in his uncle's suite with the kitchen and living room. "I'm so glad you came to meet up with me."

Later he walks over to the school with his Sheshatshiu supporters. Many snowmobiles are parked around the entrance. Giant walks in first and the others follow. A band from Natuashish plays a song about being a proud Labradorian as everybody claps and sings along. Everyone eats a good meal of caribou soup and a number of people get up to speak on the community's behalf. Each thank Giant for his inspirational walk to battle diabetes. Giant is nervous.

"I can't speak, I need you to translate for me," he says to Nikashant. "I feel very proud to see all you people," he says in Innu-aimun. "I see the momentum is building for this walk. For a while I felt like I was all alone on my walk. I was thinking nobody cares, but I see now that people do."

When he is finished speaking, the group from Sheshatshiu joins him to present the mayor with a canoe replica to thank the community for its support. Brenda Colbourne presents Giant with a cheque for more than four hundred dollars. "There's more where that came from," she says to Giant.

Finally the evening winds down. Giant and the Sheshatshiu supporters head back to the hotel. After walking for weeks and sleeping on boughs inside his tent, falling asleep in a regular bed feels very strange.

The following morning a vicious storm arrives with a skittish wind. A stellar supporter and family friend, Napess Riche, is eager to fly back home but the flight to Goose Bay is cancelled. For three days the storm rages on and for three days the group and Giant are stranded in Postville. Napess feels especially trapped in his hotel room where the window is completely blocked with snow.

As the storm settles in for a fourth day, Nikashant gets a phone call at the hotel from SOCAM, the Quebec Innu shortwave radio station. The reporter wants to interview Giant. Giant has a chat with him and a short while later he shouts down the hallway to tell Nikashant he is also wanted for an interview. In the middle of responding to a question, Nikashant is interrupted by the sound of a plane flying directly overhead.

Nikashant's wife Tsheni rushes into the room. "Hurry up!" she says. "The plane's just landed."

Postville welcome.

At Big Point, Giant towers over Postville supporters.

"I have to go," Nikashant tells the interviewer, who laughs. Nikashant and Giant are happy to know that people in all the Innu communities have heard the interviews and know about the walk.

Nikashant and the others from Sheshatshiu gather their things and head to the airport. Giant accompanies them to the airstrip. Nikashant gives Giant a last hug before boarding the plane.

"Be careful," Nikashant says to his nephew. "Stay put during storms."

"Don't worry," Giant replies. "I want you to come to Hopedale when I get there."

"I can't promise." Nikashant sees the strain on Giant's face. "Okay, I'll be there."

Giant smiles and walks away. He looks back as the plane takes off and waves goodbye. Everything is as it should be. His grandparents are happy with him.

After Matshiu Ben's death in 1977, Maniaten continued to follow her husband's dream. Despite great odds, she was determined to save the land for future generations. She knew it was now up to her to ensure that her children would know their culture. Wildlife laws angered her and she was particularly wary of the military jets training over Innu camps in the country. The laws and low-level flights were clear violations of the rights of the Innu to live freely on their own lands. Maniaten devoted the rest of her life fighting for the rights of her people. She was always at her people's side whenever there was unrest or protests to fight the injustices that had befallen her people. Giant was a boy when the Innu began to stand up for their rights. He often accompanied his grandmother on protests.

In the 1980s the Innu mastered the art of protesting when the Canadian Government struck a number of deals with NATO (North Atlantic Peace Organization) allies to practice military low-level flying over Innu lands. Overflights by these manned missiles, operated mainly by the British and Germans air force pilots, were a horrific experience for the Innu. The screaming jets flew as low as a hundred feet at speeds that could break the sound barrier. Many flights blasted above Innu camps in choice Innu hunting grounds and all over the Labrador interior.

Giant experienced one such overflight when he was about six years old. The plane flew by so low, it terrified him and his cousin Ben and they leaped through the doorway of the tent, almost running right into the hot woodstove. Another time when there was nowhere to escape the attack plane, he saw the pilot's face and trees bending along the plane's path.

Many Innu families were subjected to these overflights. Canada had agreed to allow this military flight training to occur over "uninhabited" territory. Innu leaders met many times with the Canadian government, but to no avail. In fact, the Canadian government was ramping up plans with NATO to build a superbase that would host 40,000 test flights every year and include a dozen practice bombing ranges—two for testing live ammunition. Maniaten and other elders were getting more and more worried.

The Innu were not prepared to take this sitting down. It was time to take action. They developed a number of strategies to try to gain national and international exposure about the plight of their struggle against NATO's war games over their territory. One time Maniaten took her family to camp at Minei Nipi to occupy one of the bombing ranges. Three other families joined them, as well as their friend Jim Roche, a priest who wanted to spend time with the Innu on the land to learn more about their culture. Their occupation temporarily halted practice bombing.

Around the same time, Giant's uncle Ki, his aunt Manimat, and his great aunt Nush also decided to take action. One cold fall night they crept under the heavily-guarded fence surrounding the perimeter of the Goose Bay airbase to wait for dawn when the military jets would begin their runs. At one point during the long night, military guards grazed by them as they hid behind trees. They held their breath but managed to evade detection. The sun rose and the three heard the jets' engines rev up. They got up off the ground and walked towards the tarmac waving the flag of the Innu homeland. Two jets taxiing down the main runway were forced to stop and before too long the three protesters were whisked away to jail.

Many other Innu set up camp near the Goose Bay runway. After much discussion among Innu leaders, elders, and young people, over two hundred Innu decided to take action. They made a first crack into the fence structure surrounding the entire runway and tarmac. Before the jets took off, a huge piece of the fence had been struck down and a crowd of Innu were on the runway. Elders raised their hands skyward, praying, "God, watch over us because we're only fighting for our right to protect our land and culture." Before long many were arrested and charged.

Manimat, who was involved in more than one protest, refused to sign an undertaking that said she would stay away from the Goose Bay airfield. She received the longest sentence. After a court hearing, Giant stood with Manimat's husband and three children, waving goodbye outside the gate at the Goose Bay airport as she was being transferred to the women's prison in Stephenville, Newfoundland where she would serve six months.

Over the years the Innu campaign against military flight training over their homeland got a lot of national and international exposure about their struggle. In the end NATO decided to cancel its decision to set up the superbase in Goose Bay, and the Berlin Wall fell.

The Innu organized many other protests to assert their rights. They pulled out their hydro meters and refused to pay their electricity bills, and they protested against the further damming of the Mista-Shipu. They staged more than one protest hunt against provincial wildlife laws that kept them from hunting caribou. They gained the respect they deserved from these actions. Government and industry were forced to pay attention and the Innu now enjoy more freedom to practice their culture, as well as benefits from developments on their land.

Later when the Innu would talk about these protests, they would mention how united the Innu were in their struggle. The protests renewed an overwhelming sense of pride. The Innu were one.

Giant's walk has also served to unite the Innu. Giant is very happy with the reception he received in Postville, but he is not aware of the full impact of his walk on all those who hear about it. Both friend and foe are rallying behind his dream. Family feuds and longstanding disputes in his community dissipate as he inspires everyone to rally around a common cause.

Momentum continues to mount. Plans are well underway in Natuashish to raise money for the campaign. Two women have been really inspired by Giant's initiative to create awareness about diabetes. They cannot resist the temptation to join him on his walk. Manin Dicker is a diabetic and a proud mother and grandmother. She goes to the Natuashish radio station to announce her plan to the community. She will walk to Hopedale to catch up with Giant and accompany him back to Natuashish. As she finishes speaking on the radio and heads home, her aunt Kestin Rich meets her at the door. "I'm walking with you," Kestin announces. The two pack up their gear and head out to walk the ninety kilometres south to Hopedale where they will await Giant's arrival.

Giant has been informed by satellite phone of the women's plan. He is delighted but his preoccupation at the moment is to reach Hopedale as quickly as possible. The land has become more barren. With fewer trees, he knows there will be more challenges ahead. He leaves Postville and that day manages to make it to a cabin where he and his shadow team spend the night with two hunters from Postville. The next morning, he sets off hoping to bed down that night in another cabin belonging to Randy Edmunds, a Makkovik resident. He makes it, but once again the weather intervenes and wreaks havoc on his plans. Stranded again for two days in the cabin with Napess and Anthony, he itches to be on the move again.

Morning comes again and he awakes early, very early. Before too long, he sees stars peeking through the clouds over to the northwest in the night sky. "It looks like it's going to clear up," he announces to his sleeping shadow team. He tells Napess and Anthony that he plans to set out soon to walk his hardest so he can make it to Hopedale by noon.

By the time he has packed his gear, it is 4:30 a.m. and the winds have died down considerably. He walks out onto the lonely ice towards Hopedale. As he pulls the toboggan with all his gear, he thinks about the dangers of polar bears prowling around his tent in the night before dawn. He stops often, looks carefully at humps resembling the outline of a polar bear out on the horizon. He waits to see if they move, then approaches tentatively until he knows they are only jutting ice. Relieved, he walks on across the empty icescape. He had expected the snow to be hard and smooth sailing on this part of his trek, but it proves arduous. He pushes on and each snowshoe step that scrunches down onto the ice is agonizing. He knows he must walk quickly before the winds pick up. He senses yet another blinding blizzard approaching to lord over the open ice and treeless shores.

The shadow team is barely awake, stretching and yawning by the time Giant has walked twenty kilometres, pulling his sleigh and gear, his head bowed down against the wind. The sun rises spectacular over the empty field of ice and dotted islands. The cold, crisp air turns his breath into ice crystals on his chin and bites into his cheeks. He looks out to an island beyond and figures he can reach it in half an hour if he walks rapidly, but it takes him three hours.

Meanwhile Manin and Kestin, the Natuashish women have reached Hopedale already and for two days have been waiting patiently for Giant's arrival. Today, they set out to meet up with the man. He is

Kestin Rich and Giant

Manin Dicker

expecting them. Manin catches up with him first. She jumps off the snowmobile and walks towards Giant. "Are you one of the women who wants to walk back to Natuashish with me?" he asks her.

"*Ehe* (yes)," she replies and gives him a big hug. "I'm so happy to finally meet you in person. I'm so impressed with what you're doing for us."

By the time the shadow team catches up to Giant and the women, they are only ten kilometres from Hopedale. The sun shines bright and the wind blows easy. Giant feels strong. His body has grown lean. He is more agile and tires less easily. While he can see the tall communications tower over Hopedale, he does not see Kat sitting on a hill watching over his long trek on the ice below. He grins, knowing how close he is. He gives thanks to his grandparents for their comfort and guidance.

Maniaten and her family developed a special fondness for one particular spot in *nutshimit*. In the spring and fall they often headed to Kapininien Nipi (Gabriel Lake), just south of the Mishta Shipu (Churchill River) and 120 kilometres west of Goose Bay, where they would spend up to three months living on the land. The Band Council's outpost program provided transportation. Giant was always one of the keenest to go. One time he begged his grandmother to take him out to *nutshimit*, but she told him no. She said he was too lazy and that the family would starve because of his laziness. Those words stuck with Giant for a long time. From that time on, he worked hard in *nutshimit* every chance he got. He knew his grandmother could see him working so hard. He learned to be the accomplished hunter. He made her proud.

One of Giant's favourite memories is of a plane ride to the head of Kapinien Nipi one late April day. Giant was strapped to a seat beside his grandmother, while his sister Nathalie and cousin Matshiu sat across the aisle. Maniaten was looking out the window as they approached the lake and the plane made its final approach, touched down, and came to a stop. "It's like we just landed in heaven," Maniaten pronounced. She looked forward to family life in *nutshimit*, the way it should always be. She loved the togetherness and all the laughter, the good stories about the day's hunt, and the funny things that happened along the way.

But the harassment of wildlife authorities in *nutshimit* was not so funny. Giant was just a youngster when the authorities in helicopters came and raided his grandmother's camp. He watched them confiscate all the caribou and snowmobiles. Giant was so distraught. He felt sorry for his grandmother, his aunts and uncles, and their children. He knew even at a young age that this harassment led to further dysfunction in the family, because they were being forced to live in another society.

One cold February morning in 1987, Maniaten woke her son Nikashant to tell him Innu were traveling on snowmobile south across Atatshuinapek^{u} (Lake Melville) to hunt caribou in Kamiuapishkut (the Mealy Mountains), a restricted zone. As news about the protest hunt trickled through the community, more and more people packed up their gear and left to set up tents and show support for their fellow hunters. Innu elders had

Maniaten was looking out the window as they approached the lake and the plane made its final approach, touched down, and came to a stop. "It's like we just landed in heaven," Maniaten pronounced.

decided the herd was healthy enough to withstand a limited hunt. Maniaten and her family, including Giant, were excited. This time the hunters did not sneak around. They got their caribou while the RCMP and wildlife authorities flew overhead in helicopters. One morning the authorities landed into the camp trying to confiscate the meat to use as evidence of illegal hunting. As soon as the children saw the wildlife officers, they immediately ran over to sit on the caribou. Giant sat proud and brazen. The officers left. Once the elders' quota was reached, the hunters and their families packed up their gear and headed back to the community. A number of young leaders were charged and taken to the St. John's Penitentiary. Their arrest only made them stronger and more determined. The togetherness people experienced in the camp strengthened their resolve to keep fighting for their rights.

These were good years for Giant, but Giant's world came tumbling down when his grandmother died on June 2, 1996. This was the saddest day of Giant's young life. Thoughts of despair raced through his mind. "Now that my teacher and mother is gone, what'll become of me? This is the end of our family going out in the country."

Maniaten died knowing her eldest son Shan Shushep would soon follow. Shortly before her death she visited Shan Shushep as he lay ill in his hospital bed. She felt awful about her son's terminal illness. She knew he was so afraid of dying. He was always pleading with his caretaker, his brother Nikashant, to keep him awake and not let him fall asleep. Nikashant reassured him that he would not leave him alone.

On that visit Maniaten said her goodbyes. Back home she spoke of how she never thought she would see the day when one of her children would leave this world before her. The following day she was hospitalized and she died the next morning. Before Nikashant could break the news to his brother about his mother, Shan Shushep said, "I know. Lay me back on my bed. I'm not afraid of dying now." He died exactly two months later.

Giant was the most emotional during the farewell ceremony for his grandmother. A once proud grandson who looked up to his grandmother was now terrified of being left alone in the world. He tried to be strong throughout the funeral. He was the bigger boy over his other siblings and cousins, and he did not want to show too much emotion until he found himself alone. Afterward he thought constantly about his grandmother and their happy life together. He wondered if he had the strength to carry on by himself. Confused, he resorted to a life of drugs and alcohol at a very young age. What was the point of going on without this person he loved so much? He went from one brother or uncle to another to find solace and meaning to his life. He had not only lost his mentor and grandmother, but his uncle Shan Shushep was also gone forever.

Years went by before the family felt comfortable about going back to Kapinien Nipi. Maniaten's children thought it would be too lonely to go back without her. Sometimes Giant would try to entice his uncles into going with him. "Don't worry about the wood when we go out to *nutshimit,*" he would say to them. "I'll take care of getting all the wood." Some complained about their health. They were afraid to be away from medical care. "It's time you got out of your trucks and started walking," Giant would say. "Exercise is good for you."

Finally after a long six years, the family was finally ready to return. Preparations got underway and Giant felt like he was going back home. On the plane with his family he scoured the vast terrain below thinking about his ancestors' journeys. Eager to step off the plane, he rushed to his late grandmother's log cabin. He stumbled on a watch belonging to her. It was still ticking after six years. It showed the same time as the watch on his wrist. Giant wondered how the battery could still be running. Somehow it had not frozen during all those winter months. He hung the watch up on the wall. "Nikau must still be here," he thought. He felt good. He knew the family would be returning every spring to hunt. They would again journey regularly to visit the place their mother and grandmother had always called heaven.

Giant's memories of his grandmother were very dear to his heart. She had shown him so much about helping others. She taught him to love *nutshimit* and to respect the land and the animals like his grandfather had always done.

Hopedale

As Giant, Manin, and Kestin approach Hopedale, they can see from afar that people are walking towards them. About forty children have broken away from the crowd waiting for Giant on a nearby island. The youngsters are so proud when they catch up to the trio. They want to help Giant on his last stretch. One child touches Giant's walking stick and asks him if he can carry it for him. Giant declines, saying he is afraid he might lose it amongst the crowd. He is not about to part with his magic stick that has helped him come this far. He plans to take it on future walks.

The attention again overwhelms Giant as he reaches the cheering crowd of about three hundred people who quickly envelop him in a circle. About a third are young people from the school greeting him with placards and messages of encouragement. Giant will take the placards back home to decorate his girlfriend's basement as reminders of all the support.

A feast has been planned in the school gym to welcome Giant. Giant's supporters from Sheshatshiu and Natuashish head up the hill to the school on two snowmobiles. Giant and Kat decide to walk up. As they walk through the door, the cheers of hundreds of people fill the room.

Giant walks toward the stage. People say Giant is a man of few words, but they see his actions have spoken loud and clear. When his time comes to speak, he motions to his uncle Nikashant to speak for him. Giant has done his own interviews on the radio and even on national television. He is

Kestin catches up with Giant, about 10 kilometres outside of Hopedale.

Giant poses with four sisters in Hopedale.

Giant and Kat.

fairly comfortable in one-on-one interviews, but still intimidated to speak in front of crowds. He tells Nikashant to thank them for having this feast and to tell them he really appreciates their support. Nikashant delivers the same speech he gave in Postville and countless times in his own radio interviews, explaining the purpose of the walk and how it came about. Young people perform an Inuit dance, which Giant really enjoys.

Afterwards, everyone — young people, families and elders — want to have their pictures taken with Giant. He is probably the most photographed Innu in Labrador by now. Many of the photos are being posted on the walk's Facebook site that has now attracted over 1800 members from all over the world.

The celebrations draw to a close and Giant and Kat head back to their hotel room, donated to the cause for the duration of their stay. The following morning Giant goes to the clinic to get the nurse to check a couple of blisters he developed on his last stretch into Hopedale. Walking on hard-packed snow, little did he know how large the blisters had become on his right foot. The nurse tells him to take it easy for a couple of days. A blizzard has set in, which gives him time to recuperate. The best part is that his girl Kat is there to look after him. She is in Hopedale on duty as a full-time probation officer with the Department of Justice. She decides to travel with Giant to Natuashish to be his nurse as part of the shadow team and is overjoyed when her supervisor approves her request for leave.

The blizzard stalls Giant's walk for three full days, but he decides to head out again the following day. Early the next morning Kestin and Manin wait anxiously for him. The three slip through the snow-covered streets northward onto the ice while the village still sleeps. Kat watches them turn into small dots on the horizon as they snowshoe to meet the rising sun. Giant soon realizes he walks faster than the women, but he decides that for a couple of days he is happy to take it easy and walk with them.

The wind picks up and visibility is near zero in the bitter cold. The shadow team stays close, ensuring that Giant and the two women are always in sight. For the first time, they can really see all the obstacles Giant has surmounted on this walk. They watch him push onward, with his frostbitten cheeks and legs straining against the high winds. The three walkers are very relieved to stop and thankful for all the extra hands to help quickly set up camp that night just the other side of Flowers Bay.

The next morning, Kestin and Manin awaken Giant. They peek through the door of his tent and announce to him they are ready to walk.

"What time is it?" Giant asks.

Ki Antane

"Three-thirty," the women say together. They want to get an early start because they know that they have been holding Giant back from walking his normal pace. They saw him wait many times for them to catch up.

Giant and Kat set off around 10:00 a.m. to catch up with the women. They walk a few kilometres in the bitter cold and Giant can see that Kat is working up a sweat. He worries she might get cold. He notices a snowmobile off in the distance heading toward them. The young guy from Natuashish stops to wish them well. Giant asks him to take Kat back to the camp. Relieved that his girlfriend is headed back safely to the warmth of the tent, Giant pulls out his last cigarette, lights up, and pushes on to catch up with Manin and Kestin. More well-wishers come on snowmobiles as he nears the camp.

Meanwhile in Natuashish, the interest and excitement heightens as preparations for a feast come together to celebrate Giant's dream. After five weeks of walking in unforgiving and harsh weather, through every type of snow and terrain, with and against the wind, Giant has proven he can keep up with his ancestors.

As a young man Giant often found himself out on his ancestor's land with his uncle Ki, who was really more like a brother because they were both raised by the same woman. The two often hung out together and took every opportunity to escape their lives in the village. They loved the life of hunting and trapping — to breathe the clean fresh air, to eat the day's kill, to sleep at night with a body weary from the day's trek.

Early one morning when the two of them were at Kapinien Nipi (Gabriel Lake) with others in the family, Giant woke up to the sound of Ki stuffing wood in the stove. "I must get up too," thought Giant, "It'll be a nice day and I need to tag along on Ki's long walk." As he crawled out of his bedding, he could hear the crackling fire in the stove. "Where are we going today?" he asks.

"We're going to set beaver traps over where we saw signs of them three days ago," Ki replied. Giant did not mind the long walks over streams and hills. He remembered with pride all the times he handed over his day's kill to his grandmother, even at the tender age of 12. He knew that today he would kill a few partridges or porcupines along the way. They quickly wolfed down a breakfast and headed out. Giant searched for signs of porcupine as they walked. A skilled hunter, he knew how to scour the terrain. Sure enough, he killed two porcupines along their way. They set the beaver traps and returned to camp.

Early the next morning, the two paddled along the shore to check their nets. The fish were bountiful. "This is the life," Giant said to Ki more than once that day. The following morning the two were up early again. They packed a lunch for the long journey to check their traps. After hours of walking they come across a stream, where Ki said they should stop to boil up a cup of tea and eat their lunch. Giant smiled as he sipped his tea and chowed down some bread. "If we were in Sheshatshiu, we'd still be drinking from last night because it's Saturday morning," he said. "This would be hangover day." They laughed and carried on their way.

As they walked, Ki was constantly checking for signs. He pointed out a number of small trees to Giant — trees where caribou ready to mate had scraped by with their antlers. The animals had walked this way the previous year and they could come around again each year. When they finally reached the traps, Ki was humbled to see he had caught a beaver. On the way back, Giant killed another porcupine and two partridges. It would be late before they returned to camp, but they knew they could look forward to a nice home-cooked meal and a warm cup of tea. They would proudly share their kill with others in the camp.

That night Ki lit a candle in the tent. Just before sleep was the best time for storytelling and the two often shared stories. They talked and listened long into the night as the candle shone its soft light. Each lay back in the warmth of their small tent with the wood stove burning. They reminisced about years and decades gone by and about living in their mixed-up world. When they started dozing off, Giant blew out the candle and turned over. It was a sign he was ready to sleep. He remembered the times in much the same setting listening to his grandmother tell stories about her life. "Tomorrow is a new day," he told Ki. He rolled over. He looked forward to being overcome with sleep, expecting as always the good dreams that came to him out in *nutshimit*. "Why do we get all the bad dreams when we are back in the community?" he thought as he nodded off to sleep.

Giant and Ki also shared stories back in the village, often over a beer. Giant found he could talk to Ki about his struggles. Ki understood. He had his own struggles. One night they were drinking at Ki's house, just the two of them, listening to Andrew Penashue and his band Meshikamau singing about life in the country. With each beer, the talk loosened up. Giant wanted Ki to know he was not an alcoholic, just a binge drinker. There was anger and despair in his voice. He talked about the frustration of always having to look for work. "I don't want to work in housing construction. What's the use of that?" he said. "Houses are traps that make people stay in the village. We should build houses out in *nutshimit*. People would stay out there longer and I could work out there too."

"We've been saying that stuff for a long time," Ki said. "Why don't we just do it?"

"My cousins are all more educated in the *akaneshau* (English) world then me. Look at me. No education. No direction." Giant envied his cousins. He felt shame when he thought about his life in the village. "Everybody's looking for a job now. Fewer people are going in the country each year."

"We're like all those other Aboriginal people. Disappearing. All that's left from some cultures are artifacts in a museum. I don't want the Innu to end up in a museum."

"Nikau would be proud of us, though. I know it. She'd be happy to see us out on the land living the way she taught us."

"Look at us tonight, though," Ki replied, as he took another slug of his beer. He knew tomorrow morning would come, and he'd wake up with a mean headache, looking for a cigarette. Giant too. Their money had run out. They would be taking a walk to search out their next beer to cure their hangover.

Ki and Giant knew that they and other young Innu faced an uphill battle to reclaim their pride, to walk free on their ancestral land, to live without worries that their camps would be raided and guns confiscated because they hunted the caribou that had sustained their ancestors for thousands of years. They were caught between two worlds. In the country they were energetic and efficient; in the community they were amongst the most vulnerable. When people called them drunks, they laughed and laughed. Drowning their misery was the perfect way to avoid the useless goals they saw others pursuing in the village. But the laughter masked a hurt deep inside, a hurt that had led both men to contemplate suicide.

Giant had made two attempts to end his life. The second time, he was saved when the metal wire he strung around his neck came apart from the pressure of his weight. That night he cried out to his grandmother and walked away. He did not tell anyone until much later, not Ki, not even his uncle Nikashant.

Nikashant sits in the plane with a group of supporters, including Chief Anastasia Qupee from Sheshatshiu and Chief Prote Poker of Natuashish. They are en route to Natuashish to help celebrate Giant's triumph as he crosses the finish line tomorrow. Giant's brother Gerry Gregoire greets them at the airport. Gerry lives in Natuashish because he was adopted as an infant by his great uncle Shaush and wife Shanut. He is slightly shorter than Giant, but there is a remarkable resemblance in facial features. Gerry drives Nikashant, Tsheni and Shustin the five kilometres into the community down to his place where they will be staying. They are just settling in when Tshimi Nui, a member of the local organizing committee, calls. He wants to know if they would like to go and meet up with the walkers. The group chows down a lunch of caribou meat and bannock, and quickly prepares to leave. Gerry has scrounged up enough snowmobiles for everyone.

As they drive across the terrain from the village, Nikashant is struck by the beautiful scenery. The snowmobile trail winds its way with towering hills over to the south. He imagines the bog and lichen-rich ground amongst the trees. As Economic Development Director for the Sheshatshiu Innu First Nation, he imagines a great business that could be created in Natuashish taking tourists out into the country to experience the Innu way of life. But he does not let himself ponder whether the venture is viable. His goal today is to see what he can do to support Giant, Kestin, and Manin.

Nikashant and his wife Tsheni are the last ones to leave on snowmobile. They soon realize that the women driving the other snowmobiles are way ahead. "The women are beating you," Tsheni points out over the roar of the motor.

"I'm driving slow because of my camera," Nikashant shouts back. "Yes," is Tsheni's only reply.

The schoolchildren of Hopedale meet up with Giant to walk the last three kilometre stretch to Hopedale.

About seven kilometres from Natuashish the two meet up with Kestin and Manin. The other snowmobiles have also stopped.

"We left early because Giant is such a fast walker," Manin tells the group. "We didn't want to hold him back."

They chat a bit on the ice under the clear blue sky, but the group soon climbs back onto their snowmobiles to go find Giant. The women also continue on their way. The snowmobilers drive another eight kilometres before they reach Giant walking boldly now that he knows his dream is about to come true. Nikashant turns off the engine and watches Shustin climb off the snowmobile she is sharing with Manian Nui. Shushtin hurries over to Giant, tears streaming down her cheeks. "I'm so proud of you," she says, and gives her son a hug.

"I told you I'd make it," Giant replies. "It won't be long now." The day is too cold to linger and Giant continues on his way, his left foot paining from a new blister. With every step his snowshoe rubs against the raw blister.

Manin and Kestin have pitched their tent and settled in by the time Giant meets up with them. He walks in and joy fills the air. They know this will be their last sleep before they walk into Natuashish. They plan to arrive at noon. Many curious well-wishers are driving the six kilometres from Natuashish to pay a visit with food and gifts, and to shake hands and express words of admiration.

Kestin

Napatik (Sebastian Piwas), a hunter from Natuashish, brings Giant a caribou skin jacket, decorated with two caribou heads beaded onto the back. "Now I feel like a Chief, " Giant says, as he tries on the coat. Manin and Kestin laugh out loud. "Maybe you should be," Kestin says. Giant loves the jacket and thanks Napatik. He looks over at Manin and Kestin. He has grown fond of his two companions and knows he will be back to visit them in Natuashish. They have shared some of their struggles with him as they walked together. Giant often made them laugh with his quick sense of humour.

The sun sets over the mountains and time for sleep nears. Giant invites Nikashant and Tsheni to spend this final night in his small tent. Nikashant would like to but he knows that Kat will spend the night. He does not want to intrude so he declines. Besides, the tent is too small to hold four people. Giant follows Nikashant and Tsheni out of his tent.

"Tomorrow's the big day. We should be there by noon," Giant tells Nikashant. "My grandfather will be very happy."

Nikashant senses Giant is almost in tears. Nikashant thinks about how far his nephew has come. He is impressed with Giant's determination to help people.

"I'll be waiting for you in Natuashish," Nikashant tells Giant. "That'll be the end of my job supporting you. I will be able to go back to my regular job." He knows Giant must be so proud of himself. As he hugs his nephew, his mind flashes back to last summer when he was vacationing in Quebec with his family and received a frantic call from his son Ben to tell him Giant was in trouble.

Manin

The third time Giant attempted suicide, he had a plan. This time he would not fail. He would end his futile life. Everything was all set in the basement. He hung a strong steel wire above his head, underneath which he placed a bucket. He prepared himself by drowning his despair with a few shots of hard liquor and a couple of joints. He took one last look around the basement, strung the wire around his neck and kicked the bucket out from underneath him.

He awoke on the cold basement floor and stared up at the ceiling. The wooden support from which the wire was attached had snapped from his weight. He sat motionless, tears welling up in his eyes. How could this be? He wandered upstairs, groggy and disoriented. He had to call his cousin Ben, Nikashant's son, who had always been his best friend growing up. At first Giant talked about his grandmother, about how he felt so out of place since she was no longer around. He talked on and on in anguish until his cousin began to cry.

"Hold on a second," Ben said to Giant. "I'll try to get a hold of my father in Quebec." Ben dialed his father's cell phone number. Nikashant, who was vacationing with his family in Ste. Anne de Beaupre, picked up. The voice on the other end, was panting and crying.

"What the hell's going on?" Nikashant asked.

"Giant wants to end his life," Ben said sobbing. "He's at home alone about to do it."

"Stop crying and calm down. You need to rush over to where he is. Get him to call me right away."

Five minutes later the call came in. Nikashant knew how vulnerable Giant was feeling. The two talked for twenty minutes until Nikashant could no longer restrain his emotions. After much weeping on both ends of the line, Giant said, "I want to end my life. I feel so alone and useless. Nobody in our family cares about me."

"It's not true," Nikashant said to him without hesitation. "What matters is that I love and care about you. You need to believe me." A short pause followed.

"Okay," Giant responded. "I'll wait for you." He did not like to hear his uncle's sobs. He would wait for him to come back from his vacation and they would talk some more. Giant handed the phone back to Ben, who was relieved to see that his father has calmed his cousin down.

"*Nutau* (Dad), he wants to come with me to my house, "Ben said. "I'll put him to bed."

"Okay, that sounds like a plan. Tell him not to drink anymore," Nikashant said. "I'll come home as soon as I can." He put down the phone, turned to his wife to tell her they would need to head back to Sheshatshiu in the morning. That night he lay sleepless as his family dozed around him. He wondered why so many young people were resorting to suicide, especially among First Nations people. The rate was so high.

Back in Sheshatshiu, Ben took his cousin back to the house he shared with his girlfriend. He waited to make sure Giant was sound asleep before heading off to bed himself.

To Natuashish

Giant awakes and thinks immediately how this is the big day. It has been a cold night and he was up constantly to replenish the wood in his stove. This will be a day to cherish for the rest of his life. He's made it. This is his proud moment.

Napess and Anthony, Giant's shadow team, are already packed up and headed back home on their snowmobiles on this brilliant, cold morning. They have done an excellent job supporting Giant. In each community they have been remembered and thanked in speeches, but they did not come for the recognition. Helping people and working to strengthen the Innu culture is their lifelong commitment. They want to be in Sheshatshiu for the celebrations that await Giant's return.

Giant pulls on the Innu outfit he donned when he first embarked on this journey five weeks ago. He is pleased to see that Manin and Kestin are also dressed in traditional Innu garb, much like clothing worn by their parents and grandparents long ago as they wandered their ancestral homeland. Nikashant has turned up by snowmobile to take pictures and document this important day.

As the walkers head out, Giant notices his blister has not improved from yesterday and he knows it will nag him each step to the very end. A group of children, also dressed in traditional clothing, arrive to help take his mind off the pain. The children have come to walk with him to the finish line, but first they want their picture taken with Giant. They pose alone and with the group. Nikashant obliges and snaps away again.

"We'd better be on our way," Giant says, to spur the group into action. The kids, ranging from 10 to 14 years of age, are thrilled to walk ever so proudly alongside their hero. Their colourful Innu clothes contrasts with the landscape's stark white and black. As their steps crunch into the hard packed snow, they gasp from the wind's cold sting. They march on the whole morning. Some walk quietly side by side with Giant, while others run ahead. Kestin and Manin follow behind.

Giant poses with Manin and Kestin.

Giant walks the final stretch to Natuashish with a group of Natuashish youth.

Giant raises his snowshoes in triumph at the finish line in Natuashish.

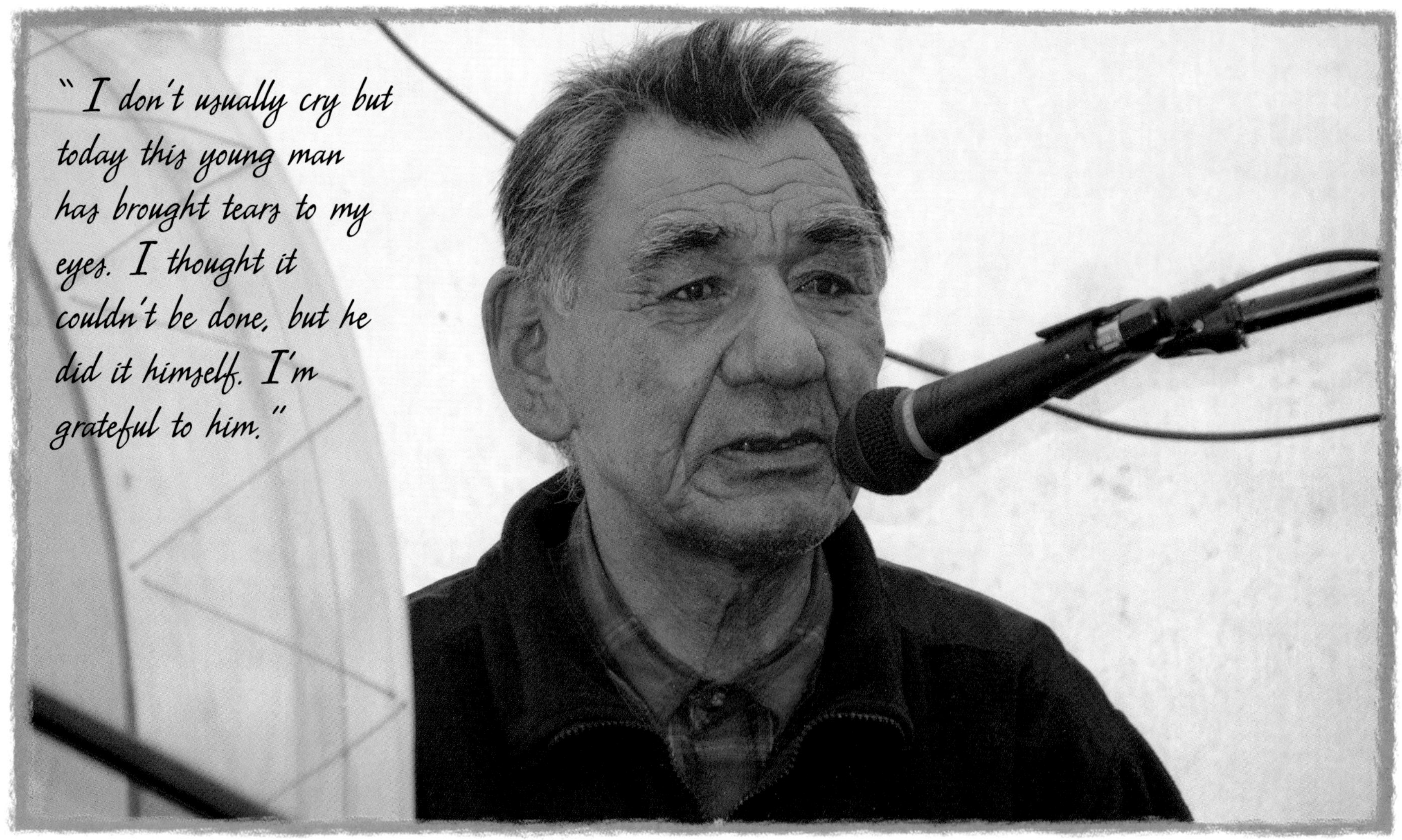

Shuashem Nui

By noon hundreds of people have gathered at the finish line in Natuashish. The talk is jovial as people await Giant and his followers. Soon a kid standing on the highest snow bank shouts out, "I can see them. They're coming!" Giant is the first to appear, followed by Manin and Kestin, and behind them the children. As Giant cuts through the finish line, he shouts out, raising his snowshoes and walking stick triumphantly into the air. The crowd roars with laughter and cheers. Many are crying as he hugs the elders first.

After everyone gets their chance for a hug or a handshake, Giant and the other walkers are led into a large tent where more elders await him. A *Mukuashan* (Feast of the Caribou) has been prepared in their honour. Shuashem Nui, a much-respected elder, begins to speak. "Your walk has brought back memories of when the Innu regularly crisscrossed this great land looking for animals to feed ourselves. I remember when I was

A CBC national news cameraman videotapes Giant and the drama of his arrival in Natuashish. Many amongst the crowd are in tears.

National CBC reporter Darrow McIntyre follows Giant with his cameraman.

"I did not walk for land claims. I walked because I care about ordinary people who suffer from diabetes. That is the whole point of my walk through the wilderness to here."

thirteen we walked to Sheshatshiu from Old Davis Inlet. My father was the *utshimau* (leader of the hunt) and there was a whole bunch of us. I don't usually cry but today this young man has brought tears to my eyes. I thought it couldn't be done, but he did it himself. I'm grateful to him."

Shuashem beats his drum and sings his dream songs about the land and the animals. The elders dance around the two stoves in an oval dance pattern. Laughter and joy fills the air as Giant and others join the elders in their Innu dance. He is deeply moved by the feast and emotional welcome. He hugs yet more people. One elder Sheshin hugs him the longest. She tells Giant his grandfather Matshiu Ben adopted and raised her when she was orphaned. She lived with his family until she married a man from Old Davis Inlet.

Giant and Kat head back to Gerry's house. As they walk on the village road, the CBC National News correspondent Darrow McIntyre and his camera crew follow behind. They have just captured the arrival and excitement of the crowd and the dance. They are preparing a documentary about the transition of the Labrador Innu from the old to the new, and they want to include Giant's story. When they arrive at Gerry's home, Darrow asks Giant about Innu land claims negotiations with governments.

"I did not walk for land claims," Giant responds. "I walked because I care about ordinary people who suffer from diabetes. That is the whole point of my walk through the wilderness to here." He does not tell the reporter that he does not think much about the whole land claims process, that what he knows in his heart is that the land he walks on is Innu and *Assimeut* (Inuit) land.

Giant with Sheshin Rich, Munik Rich and Kauashet Piwas.

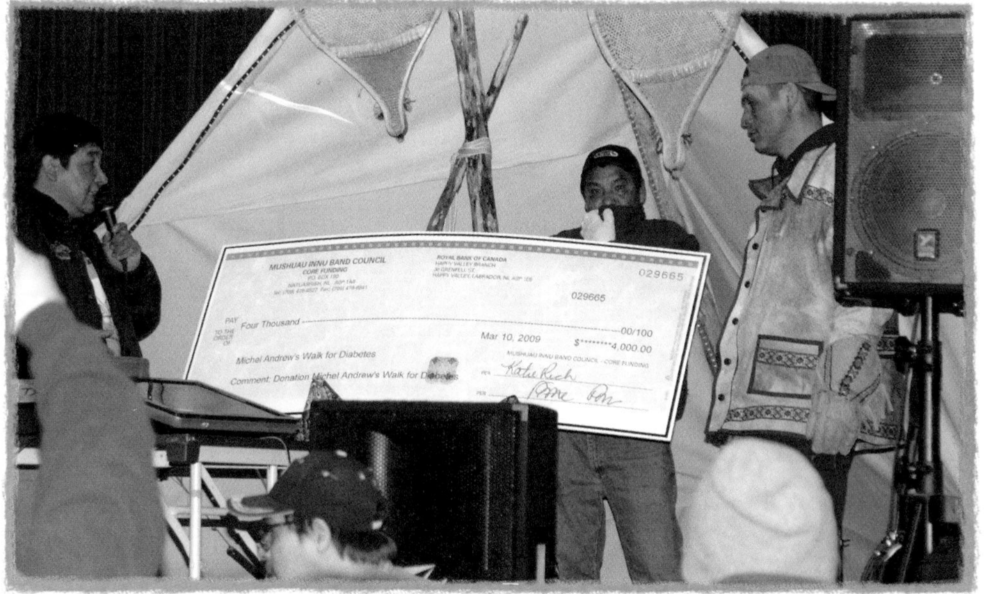

Chief Prote Poker presents Giant a cheque for $4000 on behalf of the Mushuau Innu Band Council of Natuashish.

Natuashish hosts another celebration that evening. The whole community descends upon the large modern school gymnasium. Giant feels nervous when he sees the crowd of 600, but this is no time to be shy. He walks in to a standing ovation. People cheer, "Giant! Giant! Giant!" Followed by Kat and family, he heads to the guest table. Their hosts serve a hot traditional meal of caribou, geese, partridge and lots of other good homemade food. A number of people rise to deliver speeches.

The Mushua Innu First Nation Band Council donates $4000 to the cause of diabetes and more than $6000 has also been raised by craftspeople in the community. Giant feels incredibly grateful for their support. He shakes hands with Chief Prote Poker and thanks the community for their generous donations.

The night comes to a close and Giant is dead tired. All he wants to do is head back to Gerry's and go to sleep with Kat. The next morning he pokes her on the back. "Get up. We gotta get going." He thinks he's still sleeping in a tent, and laughs when he realizes he is in a bedroom. By the time the two get up, his family has eaten breakfast and packed their bags to go home on the charter. Before Nikashant leaves, Giant reminds him that he needs the letter containing his marriage proposal to Kat. Nikashant had agreed to help him write the letter.

"I never had a chance to print it out," Nikashant tells him. "As soon as I get home, I will e-mail it to Manian Nui up here and she will print it for you before you leave."

"Okay, make sure you don't forget." Giant plans to give the letter to Kat just before they land in Sheshatshiu.

Giant's family and friends from Sheshatshiu fly home. He and Kat stay another day so that Sheshatshiu can complete its preparations for his welcome home. They enjoy the extra day to visit friends.

Innu Mikun, the joint venture between the Innu Development Corporation and Provincial Airlines, has offered to donate a charter flight for Giant to fly home and land at the spot where he started his journey near his grandmother's house along the beach road. When Giant hears the plane circling Natuashish, he and Kat head for the airport. They are joined on the trip by his brother Gerry and his family, and the elder Shuashem and his wife. Shuashem has been invited to play his drum during the Sheshatshiu celebrations. They all board the plane and Giant checks his front pocket to make sure he has the proposal letter. He wants to give it to Katherine when they reach Mokami Hill, near Sheshatshiu. He sits up front with the pilot while Katherine sits near the back. When the time comes, he hands Kat the letter.

Arriving in Sheshatshiu

Giant's plane arrives in Sheshatshiu

Giant met Kat on a canoe trip not long after Ben and Nikashant rescued him from his suicidal thoughts. He knew when he got up the morning after that fateful night that it would be wise for him to head out to *nutshimit* again to clear his head. As always, he could count on Ki to come with him and the two agreed to go on a canoe trip. Every August their aunt Tshaukuesh organized a trip on the Mishta-shipu (Churchill River) for any Innu and non-Innu protesters who were against the building of the ultimate, big hydroelectric dam on the lower part of the river. Giant volunteered each summer to help his aunt out and this year Ki would also lend a hand especially with the less-experienced paddlers on the trip.

The group headed off in eight canoes. They paddled by day and stopped in the late afternoon with enough time for the men to pitch tents and for women to collect boughs and prepare supper. Whatever kill hunted along the way was cooked up for supper. Ki paddled with a young Newfoundland woman Katherine Piercey, who was working as a probation officer in Goose Bay. Giant was impressed with this woman. "Let's change canoe partners," he suggested to Ki more than once, a big grin on his face. Ki declined, but Giant sensed this woman could be the one. He felt something he had never felt before.

Giant did not know Kat was watching him closely, how his canoe was always in the lead, how he was the one who carried the rifle and was always on the lookout for game. One day, with some prompting from Tshaukuesh, Kat brought over some supper to Giant. "Thanks," Giant said. "You're a nice girl."

Once the group reached Tshiashkueishit (Gull Island), Ki and Giant decided to canoe the whole way back to Sheshatshiu. They said goodbye to Kat and the rest of the group and continued on their way paddling another two days. They were proud to complete their journey as they neared the shores of Sheshatshiu, but Giant was not quite satisfied.

"I wish this was more challenging," Giant complained. "One of these days we should walk and paddle to Kapinien Nipi, like our mother used to do."

JVC

Giant's sister Natalie and daughter Katienna
head for the plane to greet Giant on his return home.

Giant's brother, Nicholas.

About a hundred people waited in Sheshatshiu for the arrival of the two men. Many came up to hug and congratulate Giant and Ki. One woman walked by and said, "We dare to say these guys are drunks. Look at them now. I'm so proud of them."

For months after the canoe trip, Giant kept running into Kat—at a barbeque, a wedding dance, on the road. When he was drinking he would talk to her. "Can I kiss you?" he would say. When he was sober, he was so shy he could barely talk to her. One day he asked her to go with him to the Innu Eitun Festival in Sheshatshiu. She agreed, but when he showed up drunk, she told him she wanted to get to know him when he was sober. This went on for weeks. Giant wanted to get in a serious relationship and he wanted to give up drinking. He figured this was a chance for him to sober up. When Kat asked him to move into her three-bedroom house with her, he took her up on her offer. He laughed when she told him she had two rules: no other women and no drinking. He liked to tease her about her rules. He also liked to take her hunting and snaring. Sometimes they disagreed about paying bills, getting a job, helping out around the house. Sometimes they drifted apart and Giant would go sleep at his sister's house. But he would go back and they would try again.

One night Giant brought Kat over to visit Nikashant's house to meet his uncles, aunts, brothers, sister, cousins, and mother Shustin. He explained to her how he had not been raised by his mother, but by his grandmother. The family asked her all kinds of questions. He was delighted to see that his mother seemed very fond of Kat. Nikashant showed Kat some stuff he has been writing about the family. Giant was the main character. Tears streamed down her cheek as she read his words. That same night Nikashant's wife Tsheni gave Kat a pair of handmade gloves decorated with beading and trimmed with beaver fur. She had made them herself. She told Kat she could have the gloves on one condition. Kat would have to go to *nutshimit* for six weeks with the family and learn about their way of life. Kat looked at Tsheni and then at Giant, and promised she would go.

Over the next month, Giant tried hard, but he would sometimes drink on the weekend. Every time, he would say that this was the last time. Finally he made up his mind. On his birthday he would quit. "November 15th, I promise," he kept saying to her. His birthday rolled around and he kept his promise.

Giant was cautious about his new found happiness. It did feel like it was helping him to break away from all the problems that had plagued him since his grandmother's death. There was so much about his world he wanted to share with Kat. He wanted to know about her world too, but worried that he had no education, that his English was not good enough. Kat reassured him that these things were not important. They would find a balance between their two worlds.

The love between them grew, ignited like a fire burning out of control. No water or fire retardant could douse this evolving relationship. There was so much love in the air.

Giant hands the letter to Kat, expecting her to open it and read it before the plane lands, but Kat tucks the letter into the inside pocket of her coat and does not give it another thought. She stares out of the window of the plane as it circles the community preparing for its descent.

Hundreds of people line the shores of Sheshatshiu awaiting Giant's arrival. Standing in the bitter cold, many have tears in their eyes before they even see him. Others wait in their trucks parked on the beach road. Elders are dressed in traditional Innu clothing, and some young people as well. As the plane touches down on the ice and comes to a stop, silence fills the air. Giant's daughter Ketianna and his sister Nathalie are the first to greet him. The rest of the crowd follows close behind. The door of the plane opens and the passengers step out one by one. Giant is the last to climb down the ladder. He touches the ground and holds his walking stick and snowshoes triumphantly in the air, like he is crossing the finish line once again. The crowd shouts, "Giant! Giant! Giant!" People wipe their tears as they stand in admiration of the young man who has taken such big steps to find a cure for diabetes.

Giant and Kat share a kiss.

Speech after speech follow one another over the microphone as Giant hugs elders, family, friends, and others. Kids are running around, trying to catch a glimpse of Giant. People want to hold on to him. The wind picks up, whips and swirls around the crowd. Giant's friend Deedees grabs the mike and advises the crowd that the celebrations will not be held in the large tent set up nearby. The tent is too small to hold the hundreds of people who are sure to turn up. Instead Deedees invites everyone to the gym for the celebration meal and dance to be held that evening.

As everyone disperses, Giant confides in Kat's friend Annette Michelin that the proposal letter remains unopened. "Good. If Kat had said no, maybe you would've jumped from the plane," Annette jokes. They both laugh. "I have another plan," she says. "I'll pick up the flowers."

That evening Giant's cousin Peter Penashue emcees the evening. Peter is Deputy Grand Chief of the Innu Nation, the government of the Labrador Innu. The ceremony begins, speeches are delivered, and the big moment arrives. In Innu-aimun Peter tells the story of the proposal letter and how it never got read on the plane as planned. He tells the audience the only option now is to read the letter out loud. He asks Giant and Kat to stand and hold hands facing each other. Peter reads the letter over the microphone:

Giant hugs his nikau Shustin.

Shimun Michel

Katherine,

I have asked my brother Nikashant to write this note to express how I feel about you. We discussed this when we were in Postville, and here is how it goes. One night when I was laying down getting ready to fall asleep, I gazed up at the stars through the holes in the tent's ceiling. I thought about you and how blessed I am for meeting and falling in love with you. I can't imagine not having you as my soul mate and a partner for life.

When I look deep into your beautiful eyes, I can sense so much love and affection.

The words you whispered, "I love you," when we said goodbye, were always with me on my journey through the wilds. Now that I have finished my journey for now, the thought of being together again is one that I always want to hang on to for the rest of my life. So, therefore I am asking you to marry me with the utmost honesty and love for you.

Katherine, I truly love you and I want to spend the rest of my life with you.

Your Loving Friend
Michel "Giant" Andrew

As Peter reads the last words, Kat looks up at Giant and tears well up in her eyes. "Of course, I will marry you," she says. A loud cheer erupts in the gym and again there are tears of joy throughout the room.

As the elders beat their drum and hum their dream songs, old and young people alike dance around the makeshift tables. Giant and Kat make an early exit. Many congratulate them before they walk out the door. Nikashant intercepts them too.

"I'm glad I've finished my job," Nikashant says. "Now it's Kat's turn."

As they walk away, Giant hollers, "No way, your job's not finished, I'm walking again next year."

"No comment." Nikashant replies.

Epilogue

As Giant settles back into his life after the limelight of the walk, he receives a steady stream of calls to speak to groups about his experience. The requests come from as near as the local Charles J. Andrew Youth Treatment Centre to as far away as a Vancouver Island First Nations community health centre. Giant is delighted that people want to hear his story, but the spring hunting season is short and he gives in to the call of the wild.

A few short weeks after the walk, he sits in a small bush plane heading to Kapinien Nipi (Gabriel Lake) with Kat by his side. He is eager to show her about life in *nutshimit* at this favourite place, where he always feels so close to his deceased grandmother. Kat's city parents are quite worried about her living in the middle of nowhere but Giant knows everything will be fine.

Giant no longer needs to beg his uncles to go to *nutshimit.* He is more than capable of going by himself. His survival skills make him highly adept in the harsh environment that reared him. He wakes early in the *nutshimit* morning and just follows the whims of the weather. No planning needed.

Three weeks later Giant gets a call to come home. His aunt Nishapet is terminally ill and the doctor says she has only a few days to live. For months Giant's thoughts have been with his aunt, whom he adores. When he arrives at her bedside, he leans over to plant a kiss on her forehead. He is nearly torn apart by the emotion of seeing his aunt clinging to her last breaths. After she passes on, he is relieved to know that at least she is now reunited with her parents in *nutshimit.*

After the funeral, Giant and Kat return to Kapinien Nipi for another month. He is happy to show Kat his life in *nutshimit.* They talk about marriage and children, but they do not want to rush things. They both want to get married in *nutshimit,* where they know Maniaten will be there with them to share in their happiness. Like any other couple, they have their ups and downs. Sometimes they are on and off. They come from very different worlds, but they care for each other very deeply. They hope they can find the balance between their two worlds, that they can walk together and share a long and happy life.

When they return from *nutshimit* Giant takes a five-month job as a labourer in housing construction. He saves money for a planned holiday to Florida with Kat in the fall. The cool weather is just taking hold when the two leave for Florida's warm climate. A week into the holiday, Giant calls Nikashant.

"Where are the caribou?" Giant asks his uncle.

"They are close by. I just got back from up the Churchill Road, but no luck. I heard a woman from Sheshatshiu got her caribou with a single shot. About sixty men had no success, but this woman scored."

"Maybe the women should go caribou hunting and the men can stay home with the family," Giant says. They laugh. Giant adds, "Let's go hunting when I get back."

“Sure!” Nikashant smiles. Giant is in holiday dreamland but all he can think about is caribou hunting.

One night soon after Giant returns from Florida, he pays Nikashant a visit. He wants to talk to his uncle about his plans for another walk from Sheshatshiu to Uashat (Sept Isles) by way of Quebec’s Innu communities: Pakuat Shipu, Unamen Shipu, Natashkuan, and Ekuantshit (St. Augustin, La Romaine, Natasquan, and Mingan).

“Do you think my walk last March woke people up to be more active so they can avoid getting diabetes?” Giant asks Nikashant.

“Well for one thing, you’ve really inspired Manin and Kestin to keep active,” Nikashant says. “That’ll lead more people to get moving. When Mary Lucy and her family went out to *nutshimit* after the walk, Manin snowshoed out on the land while her husband and children drove by snowmobile. And eighty-one families from Sheshatshiu took part in the outpost program this fall.”

“They must be happy out there,” Giant says. “I can see them now in their tents with their families eating caribou meat and partridges, and sharing funny stories.”

“Have you done any more planning for my 2010 walk?” he asks his uncle. “I don’t know that territory so good.”

“I’ve plotted the route on the map.” Nikashant rolls out his map. “I think it’s about 1300 kilometres—a far cry from the 400 kilometres you walked last year.” The two examine the map.

“If lines were drawn on a map of Quebec and Labrador to show Innu travel routes, it would look like the veins running through a person’s brain,” Giant says, laughing at the image. Nikashant does not respond. He knows this will be the toughest walk yet.

“You don’t think I can do it, do you?” Giant asks him.

“Honestly, I don’t know about this one. There’s going to be a lot of snow that will make it harder and longer to walk.” Nikashant is not the person walking, but he knows about fighting the elements, about unforgiving weather, about all the challenges of being out in the wilds.

”Well, I know I can do it.”

“You should head out before February 1st to make sure you beat the spring thaw. I need to talk to a lot of people before that time comes. Why don’t I organize a shadow team again, but this time for the whole way? Like in the south when people walk or cycle to raise funds for a cause, they have support teams to transport their food, water and mobile sleeping quarters. Instead of having to set up camp before sundown, the support team will pitch your tent and chop some wood for you.”

“That sounds good,” Giant says.

Nikashant tells him his friend Deedees wants to help out. Deedees has friends in almost all the Innu communities on the Quebec North Shore and he plans to call them to ask for their support. Nikashant is thrilled because he does not know many people in those communities.

The two men throw a few more ideas around. Giant wants a bigger tent this time around. Also wouldn’t it be great if he could get a partner to walk with him? Finally Giant notices Nikashant is no longer paying attention. His uncle is thinking about how impressed he is with Giant’s new

Tshan Selma

Mike Antane

Penute Antane

status. The walk has made him stronger. He has finally overcome drinking and doing drugs. He is also thankful to Kat, whom he knows has been a major inspiration in his nephew's healing.

"Looks like it's time for you to go pick up your wife at bingo," Giant says. "There's still lots of time to plan this out. Anyway that's your job. You do the organizing and I'll do the walking."

Giant gets up to leave. "See you soon," he calls out as he closes the door behind him. He knows winter will arrive soon enough and there is much to be done.

As winter rolls around the corner, Giant is pumped that he will very soon head out on another great adventure. This time he is determined to find himself a walking partner. In late November he walks over to Sebastien Rich's house to see if the boy might join him on his walk. He has seen Sebastien in *nutshimit*, how hard he works, how quick he is on snowshoes, how much he enjoys *nutshimit*. The two of them walked together one time to Minei Nipi with Tshaukeush.

"Wanna come with me on my walk next year" Giant asks the 15-year-old. "I'm leaving in February and heading for Uashat."

"Are you kidding? I've been meaning for months to ask you if I could come along," Sebastien says. "I really respect you for what you did last year. I have a hard life too. The walk will keep me busy. I want to fix my life too." Sebastien looks over to his grandmother who nods her approval. "My grandmother here never took me to Uashat, so I'm going to have to take myself," Sebastien teases her. The three laugh. Giant has found his walking partner.

But a month later tragedy strikes. Giant is not concerned about the news of a house fire in the village until he hears Sebastian's grandmother on the radio two days later. "Sebastian, please come home. I'm not mad at you. Come home now," she pleads. The police revisit the burn site with a forensic specialist and people soon learn that human remains have been found and sent to St. John's for further analysis. DNA proves that the remains are Sebastian's. Giant is devastated by the news, but says nothing. During the funeral procession, he cries out and Sebastien's cousin Eugene comes over to console him.

"I'll do the walk for Sebastien. I'll walk with you," Eugene tells Giant. Giant finds solace in those words and wipes away the tears. He realizes that he too will walk for Sebastien, and for all the troubled youth in his village.

A few days later, Giant's cousin Penute comes over on one of his regular visits. "I'm really tempted to go with you on your walk," he says to Giant.

"Think about it and let me know," Giant tells him. A few days later, Penute makes up his mind and invites another cousin, Mike, to join them. They buy the warm clothing and snowshoes required for the trip. Giant is delighted to have three walking partners, more than he had anticipated. And the wave does not subside.

Nikashant receives a phone call from Joachim Selma in Mingan to say that his 15-year-old son wants to walk too. Nikashant is surprised but he likes this development. He draws up a budget for five people, but before long the list of walkers has grown to thirteen, including men and women. Most are young and a couple of them are not so old. Nikashant plots the journey on a computer map and gathers the group to give them a pep talk. A week before they are set to leave, Nikashant gets another call. The elder Kanani (Caroline Andrew Jourdain) wants to make traditional canvas clothing for everyone.

The group gathers on the morning of their departure. Hundreds wave goodbye under the blue sky as they set out on their long journey. Everyone is pleased to see the sun shine bright, but the minus thirty cold bites and the wind is not their friend. The walkers do not mind and walk fifteen kilometres to camp halfway between Sheshatshiu and Goose Bay on their first night. The next morning they walk again in the bitter cold right through Goose Bay and stop at Tim Horton's for tea and breakfast. Sheshatshiu supporters gather in the parking lot to see them off once more as they head towards the Cartwright highway. They will camp seven times along the road before they turn off into the wilds to follow the Pishiu Shipu (Lynx River) south. By this time twenty-six people have joined the walk.

Putu Pinette

Up to this point, Nikashant drives out most days to find the walkers. What catches his attention is how Giant has naturally assumed a leadership role. His skills and confidence have grown from all his time in *nutshimit* and last year's successful walk. When anyone on this walk has an issue — a personal problem or trouble walking — he or she comes to Giant. As the group is about to turn off the Cartwright Highway, Nikashant walks over to Giant to say his goodbyes. Giant takes a draw from his cigarette.

"We'll be driving out to Uashat to meet you there. Be careful. Look after this crowd," Nikashant says. "And throw away those cigarettes. They won't help you on your walk."

"Yeah, yeah. I'll quit when I get to Uashat," Giant says, a big grin on his face. "Any other words of wisdom?"

"I'm here if you need anything."

"I know. When I get back we can start planning for next year's walk from Uashat to Schefferville."

Eskueshish Benuen

"Can we just worry about this walk for now?" Nikashant says, feigning annoyance. He knows this is not the end of Giant's dream. After next year's walk, Giant plans to trek from Schefferville to Natuashish. He will then have completed what he calls the great circle of his healing journey. Nikashant is happy to take it one year at a time.

The two men bid each other farewell. As Giant walks away, Nikashant sees his own father Matshiu Ben in the way Giant carries himself, towing his toboggan stacked with his belongings and essentials. Tears stream down Nikashant's cheeks as he remembers the once desperate young man who tried to hang himself, his only wish then to join his grandparents in the afterlife. But his grandparents had other plans for him. Now he is leading a group of troubled youth in the wilds to walk and talk with each other, to share friendship, to share their agony, and to finally console each other.

Nikashant watches as the group heads off the highway and then in single file walk along the edge of the woods. They turn to wave one last time and one by one they disappear around the bend along the snowy bank of the meandering river.

Enen Ashini

As this writing comes to an end, Giant and twenty other Innu reach St. Augustine after twenty-five days of walking through the wilderness. Their walk will end here because the spring thaw has made travel to Uashat impossible. But Giant's dream has taken root in the hearts of many and the walk will continue next year and for years to come.

Arrival in St. Augustin.

Photo Album of Giant's Journey

Giant tightens up the ropes on his toboggan.

Giant's toboggan holds his tent, stove, food and belongings wrapped in a tarp. His rifle, snowshoes and caribou skin are tied up on the outside of the tarp.

Giant's daughter, Katianna sheds a tear when her father arrives from Natuashish in a small bush plane.

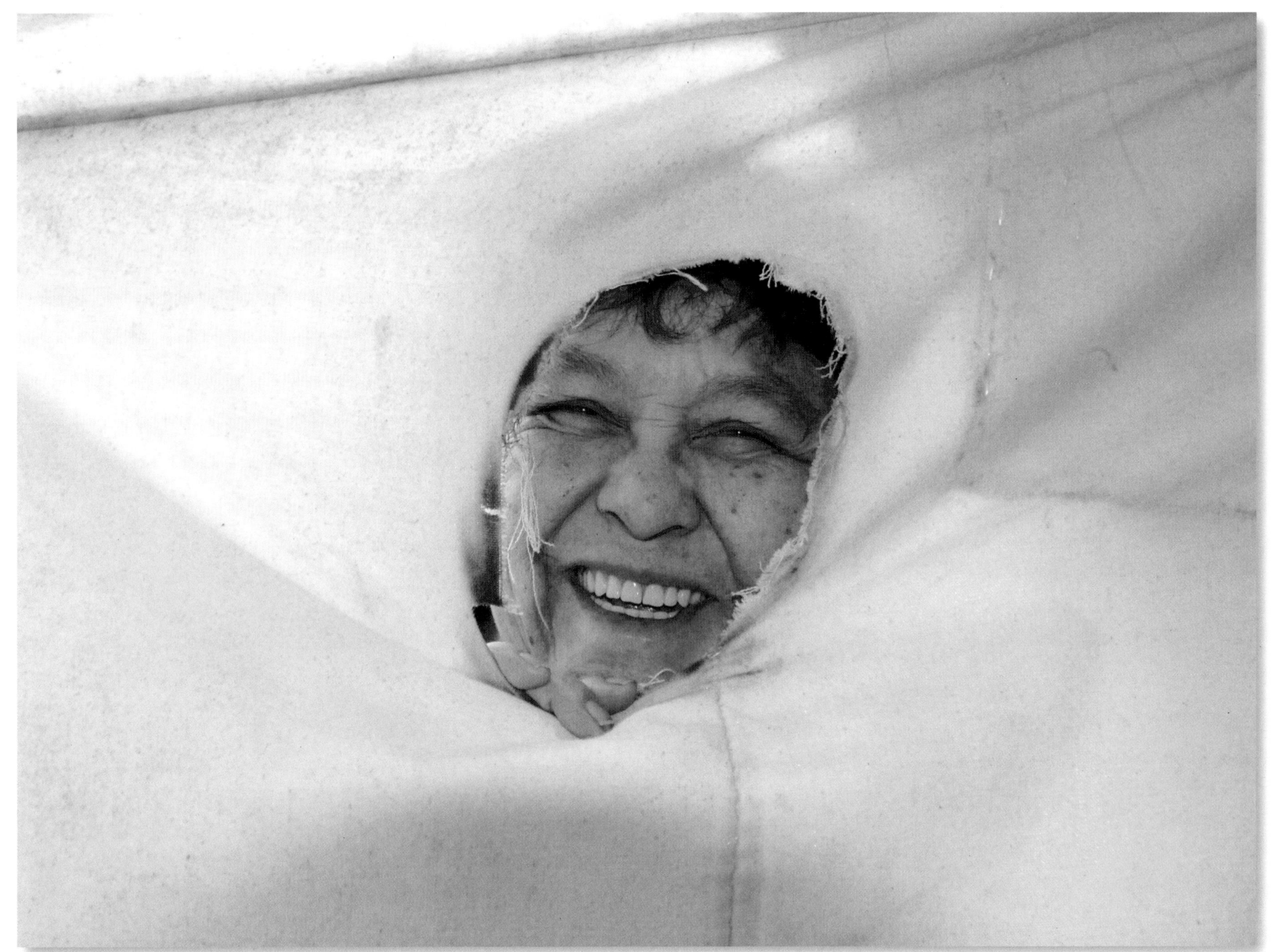

Kanani Jourdain

Giant

Anishpuas, Nikashant's son, is inspired by his cousin Giant.

Giant walking across Atatshuinipeku (Lake Melville) from his home and wellwishers.

Giant with his satellite phone. *Anthony Jenkinson photo*

Manin walking towards towering hills close to Natuashish.

At an Innu elder's request, a shadow team, Napess Ashini and Tony Jenkinson, monitor his progress.
Anthony takes this photo of Giant as he walks a very barren stretch between Postville and Hopedale. *Anthony Jensinson photo*

A group of Natuashish youngsters join Giant to walk the final eight kilometres to Natuashish.

Manin, frostbitten from the bitter wind, rests inside a tent, on the last day before their arrival in Natuashish.

Giant, Kestin and Manin and the Natuashish youth near Natuashish.

Puamun Gregoire

Uapukun Nui

Only a half a kilometre from Natuashish.

Giant, Kestin and Manin walk the final stretch to Natuashish with a group of Natuashish youth.

Giant shares a laugh with his mother Shustin.

Giant approaches the finish line, his final destination in Natuashish, after six weeks of walking in the cold, unforgiving wild country.

Manuapesh Nui

Anishpuas and Shipushis

Ben Antane, Kanapash, Anishpuas.

Giant and his uncle Aputet.

Charlotte Rich and Trevor Andrew-Hurley (Giant's brother) and baby.

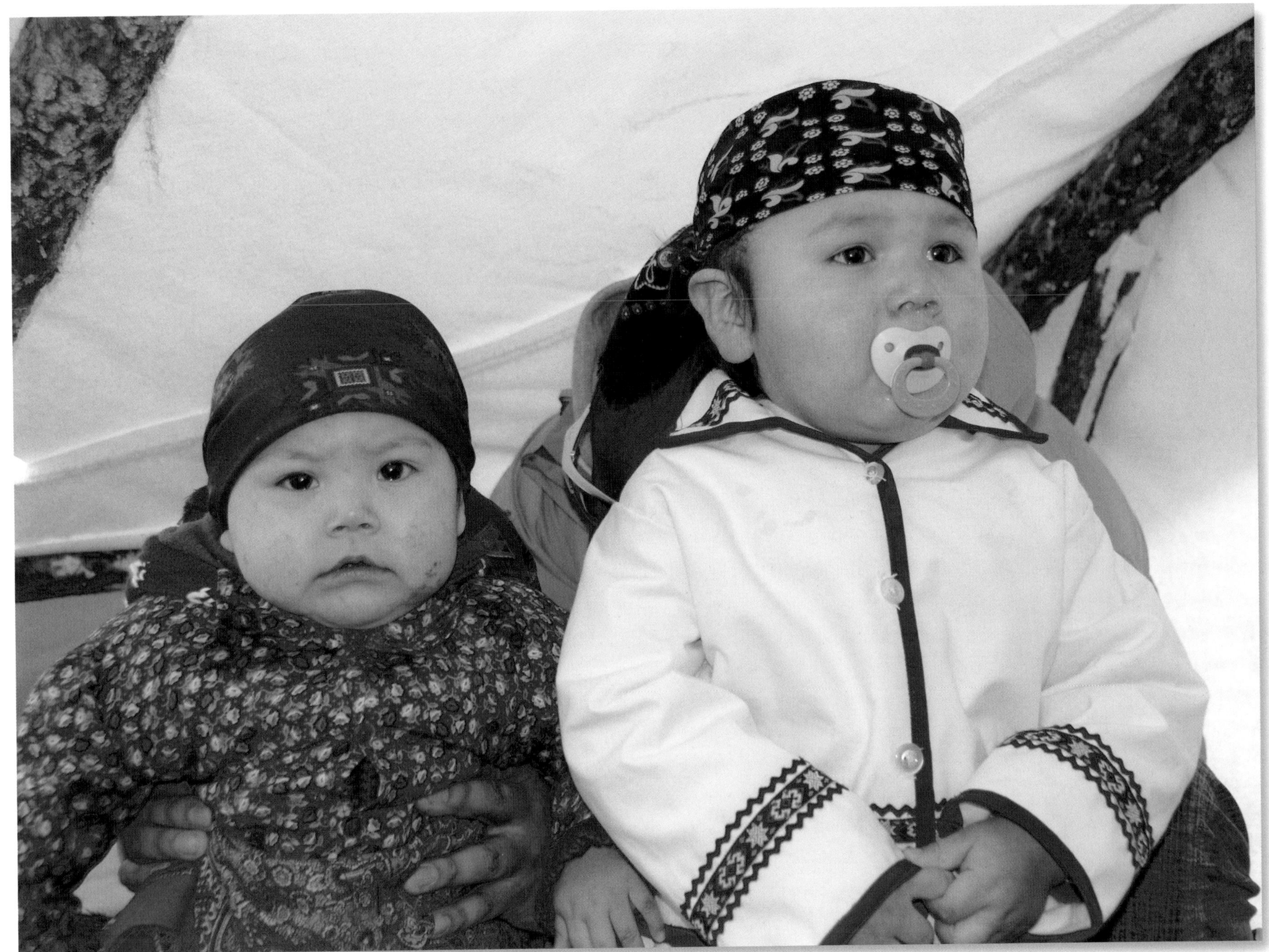

Hilary and Jayden, Nikashant's grandchildren.

Napess and Nauissau Rich, both diabetics and stellar supporters of Giant's Walk.

Giant presents a cheque for $26,000 to the dialysis unit at the Happy Valley-Goose Bay hospital.

Michel "Giant" Andrew" on the shores of Pakua Shipu during his 2010 walk.

A small husky dog owned by Kuka Benuen follows the group en route to Pakua Shipu. The small pup rode on the toboggan most of the way.

The group waves goodbye as they head off the road into the bush en route to Pakua Shipu.

This is Giant's grandmother who raised him until she died when he was 14 years old. He called her his mother.

Author Bio

Nikashant was the organizer of Giant's Diabetes Awareness Walk in the spring of 2009. He also looked after public relations. He promised Giant he would always be willing to assist him in future journeys to help others. He is an Economic Development Officer with the Sheshatshiu First Nation Band, and continues to set aside time, especially during the spring, to bring his family to Kapinien Nipi (Gabriel Lake).

PLACE NAMES FOR MAP OF NITASSINAN

Akamiuapish – Mealy Mountains

Ashuanipi – Ashuanipi Lake

Ashuanipi Shipu – Ashuanipi River

Atatshuinapek – Lake Melville

Ekuantshit – Mingan

Flowers Bay

Hopedale

Kaikopok Bay

Kakatshat Pakatan – a portage on the Moisie River

Kakuetipapukunanut – rapids on the Ashuanipi

Kamiuapishkut – Mealy Mountains

Kapinien Nipi – Gabriel Lake

Maunat – Mulligan

Makkovik

Meshikamau – Mechikamau

Meneiku – Menihek Lake

Mishta Shipu – Churchill River

Mishta Shipu – Moisie River

Mishta Paustuk Meshkanat – Churchill Road

Natuashish

Natashkuan – Natasquan

Nitassinan – Innu homeland, that encompasses much of the Quebec- Labrador peninsula

Old Davis Inlet

Pakua Shipu – St. Augustin

Postville

Sapashkuashua – hill on the north side of Lake Melville

Shimun Kapatshatauat – Where Simon Cast His Net (point near Old Davis Inlet)

Sheshatshiu

Uasha – Sept Isles

Uashkaikan – Fort Chimo, now Kuujjuak

Unamen Shipu – La Romaine

Utshimassits – Davis Inlet (Place of the Boss)

Minei Nipi

Goose Bay

Northwest River

Michelin Hill

Schefferville – Innu name

GLOSSARY

Akamakunuesht – police or person who jails people

Akaneshau – English-speaking, White person

Atshukuminsh – a bundle of belongings in the shape of a seal

Atumutakei – dog's penis

Atuminish – monkey

Kamanitushit – Shaman or Communicator with the Spirits

Kanipanikassiut – Caribou Master

Komatik – large sled towed by snowmobile

Kushapatshikan – Shaking Tent

Mishtapeut – Animal Masters

Mistnaku – Master of the Water Dwellers

Mukuashan – Feast of the Caribou

Mushuau-Innu – Innu of the Barrens, a group of Innu who lived and traveled in the more northerly reaches of their homeland Nitassinan

Namushum – Grandfather

Neueikan – dried meat

Nikau – Mother

Nutshimit – in the country or the bush

Pimin – a sacred food, prepared from bone marrow and grease for the Feast of the Caribou

Utshimau – leader of the hunt

INDEX OF NAMES

Aputet – Ben Andrew

Benuen – Benoit

Deedees – David Hart

Etuet – Edward

Giant – Michel Andrew

Ishkuess – Mary May Osmond

Kanani Jourdain – Caroline Andre Jourdain

Kauitenitakusht – Ben Michel

Kautu – Germaine Benuen

Kestin Rich – Christine Rich

Ki – Guy Andrew

Manian – Mary Ann

Manian Nui – Mary Ann Nui

Maniaten – Mary Adele Andrew

Manikatnen – Mary Kathleen Nuna

Manimat – Mary Martha Andrew

Manimatenin – Mary Madeline

Manin Dicker – Mary Lucy Dicker

Manishish – Maniss

Matshiu Ben – Matthew Ben Andrew

Napatik – Sebastien Piwas

Napess Ashini – John Pierre Ashini

Napess Riche – Lionel Riche

Nikashant Antane – Alex Andrew

Nishapet – Elizabeth Andrew

Nush – Rose Gregoire

Puna – Paula Andrew

Shamani – John Aster

Shan Shushep – John Charles

Shan Shushep – Charlie Andrew

Shanut – Charlotte Gregoire

Sheshin – Cecile Rich

Shimun – Simon Gregoire

Shimun Michel – Simon Michel

Shinapesht – Sylvester Antuan

Shuash – George Gregoire

Shuashum and Anpinamen – Joachim and Ann

Pinamen Ashini – Philomena Ashini

Shuashum Nui – Joachim Nui

Shushep – Joseph

Shushtin – Justine Andrew

Tashstu – Ann Philomena Pokue

Tenish Penashue – Theresa Penashue

Tshuakuesh – Elizabeth Penashue

Tshimi Nui – Jim Nui

Uakshakutaan – Sebastian Rich

Utshin – Eugene

Miku – Mike

Shuashem Selma – Joachim Selma